Out of Tune

ROY GATEHOUSE

Privately Published

Privately published by the author:
Roy Gatehouse
33 Salford Road
Marston
Oxford OX3 0RY

Copyright © Roy Gatehouse

All rights reserved.
No part of this book may be produced
stored in a retrieval system, or transmitted,
in any form or by any means, or otherwise,
without the prior approval of the publisher.

ISBN: 0 9543114 0 X

Published 2002

Printed in Great Britain

*To my wife Barbara,
for her
encouragement and support*

Contents

	Foreword	vi
	Introduction	vii
	Acknowledgements	viii
Chapter 1	*From Dover to Oxford*	1
Chapter 2	*Putting Down Roots*	5
Chapter 3	*Get in the Queue*	12
Chapter 4	*Chuck Him Out!*	14
Chapter 5	*Meetings*	19
Chapter 6	*Trotsky's*	24
Chapter 7	*Elections*	28
Chapter 8	*Shop Stewards*	31
Chapter 9	*Barricades*	34
Chapter 10	*Discrimination*	37
Chapter 11	*In Office*	39
Chapter 12	*Dream World*	42
	Visual Reminders	49
Chapter 13	*Another Strike*	73
Chapter 14	*Downing Street Comments*	76
Chapter 15	*All Change*	81
Chapter 16	*Victimisation*	85
Chapter 17	*A Triumph from Honda*	90
Chapter 18	*A Downward Spiral*	95
Chapter 19	*Mistakes Repeated*	99
Chapter 20	*Reflections*	103
Chapter 21	*More Publicity*	111
Chapter 22	*Finally*	116
	Name Index	120

Foreword

This book is about Roy Gatehouse who challenged the authority, opinions, credibility and motives of the trade union leaders at the Leyland factory between 1968 and the early 1980's. He did so openly and without departing from his firmly held view that trade unions were a sound and vital element of British society He displaced a particularly irresponsible department shop steward by contesting an election and winning a healthy majority.

At about the same time he wrote his first of many letters, to the editor of the Oxford Mail, all of which, with perhaps the exception of one, were published. The letters were nearly always questioning the activities of the union leaders.

Cheerfully scorning all efforts to stifle him, he took full advantage of his duty and constitutional right to attend, not only his own (Engineering) union shop stewards meetings but also the joint shop stewards meetings. That included the dominant Transport and General Workers Union. These joint meetings would be attended by upwards of 250 shop stewards, representing thousands of workers, and in the early meetings, he was in a minority of four when challenging the platform.

The history of the Cowley car assembly factory, on the old Morris Motors site, leads up to the time when the most powerful union figure, Alan Thornett, who was eventually dismissed by the company and betrayed by the people who for years blindly supported him. By then, he and his kind, had done incalculable damage to the Leyland car factory at Cowley, whilst spreading to other industries, all in the cause of his 'Walter Mitty' world of a revolutionary fantasy.

Roy was of the opinion that the masses of workers thought they were striking for more money, less working hours and to defend a hero who was fighting on their behalf. Nothing could have been further from the truth.

Introduction

'Out Of Tune' symbolizes a brief, sometimes humorous reaction to a book titled 'Inside Cowley'. The author of that publication was Alan Thornett. My story is openly provocative, forthright, and to the best of my knowledge, completely true. I also express my opinion on many of the issues raised, and most of the people I refer to, or quote are still out and about up to this time, others are deceased. Thornett was a leading shop steward at the old Morris Motors Works, which later became known as The British Leyland Car Assembly Plant. He was the driving force in the twenty five year conflict between the trade unions and the management at the factory, from 1959 through the 60s, 70s, up to 1984. I say humorous because some of his fanciful and egocentric behaviour and political objectives were just plain daft.

'Out Of Tune' touches upon the intimate, personal, family and social side of factory life, part of which was the experience at Cowley of the prolonged concern at the prospect a total collapse of the the local car industry. Fuelled I must say, by the constant prediction and speculation by the community at large, not if, but when the closure would come about. It took from 1957 until 1968 for me to realise that I could represent the union members in my own department, better than the person who at that time was my shop steward. I was nominated, stood in a ballot, and in 1968 was voted in as the Tuning department shop steward.

I was totally motivated by self-interest, in as much that it was my livelihood, until I retired, that was my first priority. I ceaselessly opposed, exposed, argued and condemned the excessively militant union leaders. Alan Thornett had said he would lock me up if he had his way, when all I wanted was for them to stop what they were doing. I opposed them holding office, and campaigned against him in elections. Belatedly it was trade union officers, locally and nationally that softened their opposition to the company's decision to dismiss Thornett on the grounds of breaking company rules while at work. My final thought is, why in each case, did the unions at national level, and the company, allow these difficulties to destroy the industry, before they took the necessary steps to stop the rot?

Roy Gatehouse

Acknowledgements

I would like to thank the following organisations and individuals for allowing me to use their material.

Oxford City Council
Lord McCarthy of Headington
The M.S.F. Union
The A.S.T.M.S. union
M.G. Rover Group
Mirror Group Newspapers Ltd
The Oxford Mail & Times
The Oxford Journal
Courier Newspapers, Oxford
Harry Landon
Jane Thompson
John Finlay
David Buckle
Bernard Moss
Bill Roche
Kay Gatehouse

CHAPTER ONE

From Dover to Oxford

*1940: Evacuated to Somerset. • 1949: Conscripted into the Army.
1952: I move to Oxford taking a variety of jobs.
On the line at Morris's.
Eight hundred of us made redundant.*

'For most of this century, the car industry has been a major source of employment for workers in and around Oxford. Before the First World War Oxford was a small market town, almost completely dominated by, and identified with, the University. In 1911, just two years before Morris opened his first car factory at Cowley, about a fifth of the towns workforce was employed in manufacturing industries. Less than twenty years later, the Citys population had doubled and a fifth of the workforce worked in the local motor industry alone. Morris Motors, and the Pressed Steel plant close by, had come to dominate manufacturing in Oxford very quickly and employment in car production doubled again by the outbreak of World War Two.
(See acknowledgement section, Ref. Lord McCarthy's *The Future of Cowley*, enquiry report).

In the spring of 1940, just before my tenth birthday, my two older brothers and I were evacuated from the Dover area to Midsomer Norton in Somerset. Our parents gathered from the newspapers and the radio that there was a possibility that the Germans, having advanced across France, capturing Dunkirk, Calais and Boulogne, were about to cross the English Channel. We were to stay with relatives in Somerset. Fifteen months later we returned to Kent. The war was by no means over, but the threat of invasion was pushed into the distant future and fortunately never happened

In 1949 I joined the Army as a conscript and in October of that year set off from Liverpool in a 14,000 ton troop ship, to Athens in Greece. After passing on to Mogadiscio in Somalia, Khartoum in The Sudan and back to Port Tewfik, at the southern end of the Suez Cannel, I arrived back in Britain in August 1951. It was an experience I have treasured ever since, although there were times when, given the chance, I would have shortened that experience. By March 1952 I missed the independence that living away from home allows, and decided to move away. Having worked with a person who originally came from Oxford and, almost as though guided by fate, I thought Oxford was as good as anywhere. On the spur of the moment I decided to make the move. I arrived in Oxford, found work and accommodation in 'digs' and have lived here ever since.

2 OUT OF TUNE

I was warned by local people not to work at the car factories, although they had been running continuously since the end of the war – six years or more. It was predicted that, eventually, the fluctuation in demand for cars would go back to being seasonal, as it was before the war, when workers were sent home without pay, in the middle of a shift, and told to stay out, until they were sent for. For a while I stayed with local garage work.

By 1953 I fancied travelling around and took a job with B J Henry, the car delivery people. In those days most of the cars were delivered or collected by road, driven that is, some by rail and a few by car transporter. We, the deliverers, would report for work at anything from 4.45 a.m., depending on the destination. Having delivered the car, the normal method of return was supposed to be by public transport, but, to boost our meagre remuneration, we would hitch hike and pocket the travelling expenses. The job was by no means boring if it was judged by its spread of destinations. The 4.45 a.m. start was to deliver cars to Hull docks for export.

When there were large consignments we would travel in convoys with a supervisor leading each one. This system sought to prevent individuals from speeding, which was a great temptation, also, in those days, new engines had to be 'run in', which meant not to 'over rev' them, by exceeding 50 miles per hour, until 500 miles were on the speedometer. On one occasion two deliverers got a lift in a sporty car driven by someone who enjoyed travelling at speed, whilst having little regard for speed limits etc. As a precaution, he got his new passengers to keep a lookout for any 'coppers' that might be about. What he did not know was that his passengers were off duty policemen, engaged in the frowned-upon activity of moonlighting when off duty. The policemen were just as interested in saving the driver from being caught as the driver, and made very good lookouts.

Having started the job in late autumn, I soon found out what it was like delivering vehicles long distances in winter conditions. Before the advent of motorways, travellers planned their journeys from town to town, and that meant 'through' most towns and cities. We would go from Oxford, through Banbury, through Southam, through Rugby and through Leicester, like that all the way to Hull. There were very few by-passes in those days, and no motorways, which not only made travel slower but meant greater distances. The route tended to meander off a bit to the West to one town and then to the East to the next, when the desired direction was to the North. Hull was 190 miles from Oxford. When the car was an MG two-seater sports model, (TF soft top - a beautiful little car and wonderful to drive), with the hood stowed away, and only the front windscreen to protect the driver from freezing fog, and having to contend with icy roads, in darkness, and on the road at 5.00 a.m., then one had to like the job to do it. There were men and women drivers, some retired, and they just got on with it. On the Hull trip, when there were sufficient drivers to warrant it, a coach from Marston Coaches in Kennington, used to be sent to the destination to bring us back to Oxford. For this arrangement we were paid 32 shillings 6d to deliver the car and 2 shillings 6d to maintain employed status while on the coach, for insurance purposes. We would arrive back in Oxford 14 hours later, for the princely sum of £1.15 shillings, (£1.75p), that was before the unions had negotiating rights in the main factory, let alone small firms like B J Henry.

There was a lot more to the B J Henry job. It was easy and pleasant but after four months I tired of it and took a job with British Road Services, Prestcold Division, as a long distance articulated lorry driver, delivering refrigeration units the length and breath of England, Scotland and Wales. One almost unbelievable fact was that the top speed of my small articulated lorry was 33 m.p.h., so different to the 14 to 20 wheeled, 44 tonne, 70 m.p.h. juggernaughts that pound our highways today. Fate intervened in my life after six months of lorry driving when I tipped my lorry over on the Woodstock roundabout, damaging all the refrigeration units, valued at £3,600. There was no other vehicle involved. I wasn't unnerved by the accident, or anything like that. In fact, the general policy of foremen in charge of professional drivers in those days, when a driver had such an experience, was to send him out straight away so as to avoid loosing his nerve and possibly ending his career as a driver. On the day after my accident I was sent on a two-day round trip to the Grimsby area, and, as always, I had a drivers mate with me, to assist with the unloading etc. Without any difficulty we set off, and had settled into the journey and were chatting away, quite relaxed, when, suddenly, when driving round a slight bend, I felt the lorry lean out and I nearly jumped out of my skin. That was the first sign of trouble at the time of my accident, and momentarily I thought it was going to happen again. We both laughed, and that was the only after effect I ever had.

When I was called in to face the depot manager, in the company of Jack Thomas, the T&GWU district secretary, he said that if I worked for him for the rest of my life I could not make good the loss involved, and gave me my marching orders. I didn't fancy my chances of being offered another lorry driving job with an item like that on my record, so, out of necessity, I took the plunge, applied and got a job on the production line at the Morris Works.

I shall always remember, having survived the interview with the personnel employment manager, at Morris Motors Cars, being sent over to the erecting shop to be interviewed by Mr Adams, the foreman, whose office was on a bridge that spanned the production lines. It was accessed by a long ramp one way and by a flight of steps, from between the production lines, the other. While waiting to be called in, I looked over the rail, down at the production lines, to see the frenetic activity and to hear the scream of the high-pressure air tools that turned and tightened the screws, nuts and bolts. Those noisy power tools were designed to do the job quickly and enabled the workers to get more work done each minute of the working day, that meant more pay at the end of the week, that is why it is called piecework. I got the job on the Morris Oxford line and started the following Monday, at 7.15 a.m.

I knew it was going to be difficult, having to adjust from driving long distances through the summer and being my own boss while on the road, and now having to buckle down to miserable late autumn weather in a factory that seemed like a prison. The relentless pace was unbelievable, in those days the production line hardly ever stopped, if it did it was mostly for minutes or part thereof, which meant we were all dependant on a 'toilet relief', who was also timed on a so many minutes per worker basis.

The pay nearly doubled my previous income and, it being a five-day week as opposed to a five and a half, helped me to stick it out initially. However, after a couple of weeks I thought it was too much. I would go to work in the morning and think to myself 'I will give my notice to leave at lunch time', come lunchtime I'd think, 'No, I'll finish the day'. The next morning I would think the same, 'I'll give my notice today at lunchtime', still miserable but I would stick that day out. That went on for a while until one day it occurred to me that I was no longer planning to leave and, as four months had gone by, I realised I had mastered it.

It would be remiss of me to give the impression that those early days were all misery and boredom. A regular bout of humour will always surface where lots of people are thrown together. Pieceworkers often operate in groups of two or more, so it was with me. I worked with one other person and we had a list of timed operations, which we shared equally. One day, when my partner was absent, a regular relief worker stepped in to do his part of the operation. This particular relief person was a bit on the lazy side and used to dodge as much as he could, sometimes at the expense of his fellow workers. On the day in question, when he arrived to start work, he asked which part of the operation was he expected to do. I identified the tasks that were his, and, for good measure, gave him a couple of my tasks as well. So he started, and I helped by demonstrating one or two of his tasks, which pleased him. When he became aware of how much he had to do, by which time he was sweating profusely, he commented on how hard my partner had to work. He said he knew some people did have lots to do and that is the way it was sometimes. I told everyone around us what was going on, and let him sweat for most of the day. I then started to show him some compassion and offered to do a few of 'his' tasks. Once again I was a decent, helpful guy in his view, that was until I told him they were my jobs anyway. He didn't seem to know whether to laugh or explode with anger, much to the amusement of those around us.

Twenty-two months after I started, due to a sharp drop in export orders to Australia, plus government intervention, a turndown in demand for cars lead to eight hundred workers being made redundant. A few weeks pay in lieu of notice and I was out of work. Was that advice, not to work at the car factories, coming true? No, the redundancy situation was short-lived and all except a few were recalled on an unbroken service clause as the result of organised trade union pressure.

CHAPTER TWO

Putting Down Roots

---
*I return to the factory and become a 'Tuner'.
Ten years later, I am elected as the Tuning Department shop steward.
An unofficial, campaigning, organisation is established.*

'After the Second World War, growth at Cowley continued almost uninterrupted for nearly 30 years. By 1973, more than 28,000 people were employed in motor and related manufacturing activities in Oxford, the vast majority at Cowley. That represented almost double the numbers employed in the early 1950s, with 45 per cent of the City's workforce involved in vehicle production in the 1960s (see page 50).
(See acknowledgement section, Ref. Lord McMarthy's *The Future of Cowley*, enquiry report)

Having first been warned by the locals not to work at the car factories because of the unreliable nature of their employment, I ignored that advice and took the job, only to be made redundant twenty two months later, I resolved to stick with local garage work for a living and turned down the invitation from Morris's, to go back to the factory. I did not respond to the invitation.

Within eighteen months, I had met and married Barbara, set up home, and created an urgent need for a better paid, job. The solution was never in doubt. To return to the factory was my best option. Originally it was to be for as long as it took to meet the needs of family life - for a couple years perhaps. The thought of going back to repetitive production work on a moving line was horrific. As needs must, I made enquiries and found they were taking on people as mechanics in the Tuning department, working in fully equipped, individual bays. I applied for a position and, with a clean record from my previous time at the factory, got the job and on the 27 December 1957 I started what turned out to be a twenty-three year stint as a Tuner.

In the eighteen months, between the date of my redundancy and the date of my return to the factory, the trade unions had gained a foothold in a move towards official recognition by the management, and a closed shop, which meant compulsory union membership (and thereby control of the members).

From the end of 1957 until 1968, I was content to be in the tuning department. In those days, there was a degree of mutual respect between the management and the workers, despite the application of strict rules and some discipline, there was still a place for the departmental Christmas party which enabled middle management and foremen to socialise for an evening. There were also dances and the occasional Sunday map reading and motor rally, all a small part of the rectification department and factory life.

However all good things come to an end, and gradually the push by the workforce, for better working conditions, a shorter working week, more pay, holidays, and a host of other things. All involved claims by the trade unions. That meant negotiations, disputes and strikes. The trouble was, there was literally no end to the struggles, the factory gradually became an industrial battlefield. Paternalism was ejected and ruthless power struggles took both its place, and its toll. In those ten years the experience and consequence of frequent disruption, prompted me to develop an interest in the trade union movement. I joined a training course for shop stewards at the local Workers Education Association.

At that time there was a Quality and Reliability Year campaign (see page 51), designed to promote interest and commitment by the workers. Every factory in the combine was to participate and every department had to form a sub committee of volunteers. They would elect a chairperson to organise activities suggested by them. The 'chair' of each sub committee would be a member of the main QRY committee. A member of the management chaired the main body. I was elected chairman of our sub committee.

The campaign boosted participation in the existing suggestion scheme, ran all sorts of competitions, laid on visits to each other's factories, held a Miss QRY beauty contest, the winner to attend functions and promotions. A monthly design-a-poster competition threw up some very talented entrants and, towards the end of the scheme, a best departmental 'display stand' competition was organised and our display was awarded third prize. Whether the campaign was a success or not is impossible to say and difficult to assess, one thing I did notice, some people distinguished themselves and thereby gained promotion.

With my shop steward training underway and the experience of representation on the QRY scheme, my ambition was beginning to take shape. One of the Tuning department workers nominated me for the position of shop steward and, as the annual election was due, I accepted, and allowed my name to go forward. I won, and took office immediately. Instinctively, I felt there was a less damaging way of conducting the relationship between bosses and workers. As it was a factory wide problem, I became aware that my position as a Department Shop Steward, required me to attend my union Shop Stewards Committee meetings, also the Joint Shop Stewards Committee, the latter being attended by upwards of two hundred and fifty shop stewards, representing thousands of workers. The first Joint Shop Stewards meeting I attended was something of a culture shock. In a debate that touched upon the unequal divide in wealth between the rich and the poor, a loud gravel-voiced steward embarked upon a tirade, citing Princess Margaret, in the crudest of terms, as an example of a privileged hanger-on of the system. That point, I decided, did not require my attention.

However, I wasted no time and when I noticed there were stewards present from a department that had been detached from the main factory and was under another authority, I made no secret of the fact. The stewards involved were a vociferous lot and to get them removed from the main factory committee would be a good way to tackle the problem of excessive militancy. I raised the matter through the chairman and was told that by rule it required that I draw up a notice of motion (see page 52), backed by the signatures of ten shop stewards and submit it to the Joint Shop Stewards sub committee, which I did the following day. My motion *'that at Morris Motors' JSSC meetings, recommendations from the platform and resolutions that directly concern only Austin Morris Cars No's 1 and 2 factories, should not be spoken to, or voted on, by members of BMC Service Division'*. Among the people who signed my motion were two ex-senior stewards and one deputy senior steward. Within a week I received a letter saying that my motion had been considered by the JSS sub committee and rejected. (No new upstart was going to push them around!) However the change was made. The BMC Service Stewards set up their own factory JSS committee. To be fair, it would probably have happened anyway. I was not to know that at the time.

I started writing letters to the Oxford Mail just after becoming a steward. The gist of my first letter, being a bit brief, said, *'If the consequences of all the damaging strikes and disruption at the factory was to cause the downfall of the company, the unions will be asking, whose fault was that?'* That letter was published in late 1969 and it brought forth the first of many rebukes from Alan Thornett who came to prominence by being elected to the position of deputy senior steward.

Nothing I was doing was having an actual effect on the level of disruption. In reality, militancy was in ascendancy and was to be so for a very long time. But I was building a base for the future. I continued to write letters to the Oxford Mail and to challenge the excesses of militancy at my Branch, at my union Shop Stewards Committee and at the Joint Shop Stewards Committee. At one of the JSS committee meetings, Bobby Fryer, who was the main speaker on the platform, criticised me for conducting my campaign through the local newspapers. He said it was an internal factory matter and I should recognise it as such. I said nothing at the time but decided to suspend that practice for a while and continue my efforts through internal union channels.

This was in no way a climb-down on my part. I knew that it would take massive public concern and condemnation against what was happening inside the car factories. A sudden collapse of the manufacture of cars would devastate Oxford's employment and business interests.

A friend of mine by the name of Michael Denver, (now deceased), a fellow shop steward, urged me to set up an organisation that would harness the groundswell of opinion among the workers to oppose and expose the unrepresentative activities of the senior union leaders. We all suffered from despondency and incredulous disbelief at what was being done in the name of democracy and workers' control. I had previously declined to do as Mike suggested saying that such an organisation would be vulnerable to infiltration by revolutionaries and rendered unworkable. This time, agreeing that the aims were sound and the need was urgent, I aimed to avoid the infiltration problem by confining the control of the proposed body to a small number of trusted and reliable people. This was clearly the way to go and I knew exactly who to enlist as our first recruit.

Harry Landon was a Tuning department store man, a close colleague who served our department for many years, and he and I often chewed over the problems caused by the union agitators. Next, was Philip May, an inspector who worked in the same building as Harry and myself. The third was Brian Jackson, a production worker on the sub-assembly section of the Maxi line. Brian was a member of the T&GW Union and volunteered in response to my open letter, the one that floated the idea of setting up 'The Organisation to Represent Moderate Opinion in Trade Unions' - known as ORMO-TU.

Having made the decision to go ahead with the project and recruited the helpers, I wrote to Malcolm Young, the District Secretary of my union, the Amalgamated Union of Engineering Workers (AUEW), and informed him of my intentions. He replied with two letters. The first was formal, on headed AUEW paper and the other was hand written on blank foolscap. The official letter cautioned me on the risks I was taking and advised me of the rules of our union with regard to the official function and procedures. The other letter went as follows (see page 50):

Dear Brother Gatehouse, Supplementary to my official letter enclosed, as you are aware, in my personal capacity I am a member of the 'Engineering Voice' Oxford Committee, which I prefer to term a progressive organisation working towards socialism with the idea of encouraging mass participation of workers towards achieving that aim. I thought it best to add this note because I do not feel I could insert same in an official letter, yet at the same time I did not wish to give any false impression about my personal membership of this unofficial committee. Yours fraternally Malcolm Young.

The trouble was I could never see any difference between the policies of Engineering Voice and those of the Communist Party. He may have desired to have more members in the engineering union but his whole problem was that he spouted nothing from the roof tops, but was more than happy to have as many communists as he could on the district committee. He was a member of the Labour Party until Neil Kinnock was leader of the opposition, then he allowed his membership to lapse and has not renewed it since, but was happy to observe us on District Committee grant £250 to the local Labour Party funds at General Election time. It was always Communist Party policy to support Labour at election time, when there was no Communist candidate standing.

My next step involved buying a second-hand duplicating machine and a filing cabinet for £35, reams of paper, tubes of ink and stencils. We were in business and ready to go! The duplicator and filing cabinet were my property and to be retained by me. I then composed an open letter addressed to 'The Assembly Plant Employees' signed it and gave my working location within the factory and my home address (see page 51). I produced 500 copies and stood at the factory gate handing them to the employees as they arrived for work.

Before I could get back to my workstation, people were coming from all over the factory, offering help and asking what I wanted them to do. I asked them to make collections to finance the production of leaflets. Following this excellent response from the people who had heard about or seen my open letter, I composed and produced 1500 copies of the first edition of the ORMO-TU leaflet. I also invited the three helpers to my home in Blackbird Leys for our first meeting.

At that meeting an agenda was drawn up as follows:

Item 1.   To consider the response to my letter, by the employees
Item 2.   To plan in detail the distribution of the leaflets
Item 3.   To promote and assist with fund raising by organising collections

Each item was dealt with and each helper took his allocation of leaflets. Distribution started the following morning at the factory gates, thirty minutes before starting time, to catch the early arrivals. It was an exciting development. The open letter had already prompted the T&GWU senior stewards to declare that they would not attend any joint union meetings with the management if I were present. This meant they would withhold all support for my constituents with any grievance that we wanted taken up. It was a toothless threat because we could meet the management on our own, at any time to sort out any problems that might crop up. At that time the Tuning department people were a passive group of workers because of the way the department operated. The production workers would have given anything to swop places with us, just to get away from the repetitive conveyor system.

The excitement I refer to was heightened by the T&GWU senior stewards public response to my open letter. The Oxford Mail published a lengthy article with bold headlines. '*Union shuns moderate group at car plant*', and went on to say '*The Transport and General Workers Union is to boycott any meeting attended by a member of the Amalgamated Union of Engineering Workers, which has set up an organisation aiming to represent moderate shop floor opinion at the Assembly Plant.*' The article continued – '*a new group, which calls itself the Organisation to Represent Moderate Opinion on Trade Unionism, has been set up by Roy Gatehouse who works in the Tuning department.*' Branch News, the journal for 5/55 branch of the T&GWU, attacked ORMO for being anti democratic and aimed at removing or undermining properly elected representatives. *Branch News* was edited by Mr Alan Thornett, the deputy senior steward for the T&GWU.

Genuine concern was voiced to me by a significant number of people who were afraid that I was trying to set up another trade union in opposition to those unions that already existed. These fears were totally unfounded. In the first edition of the ORMO-TU leaflet under the heading '*The Aims of the Organisation*', it said it was *'to support the official trade union movement and its ideals'*. It was difficult to see how much clearer it could be expressed. I was confident, as time went by, that I could adequately demonstrate our intention to stick to that rule, hard and fast.

It would be easy to claim the launch of ORMO-TU was an instant success and that it was almost unanimously applauded. But that was too much to expect. After all, the unions had extracted massive improvements in working conditions, pay increases, a shorter working week, extra weeks holidays, extra days holidays, redundancy payments and a multitude of other benefits, which brought forth continued support from the membership. The support for the moderates was based on resentment of the way certain trade union leaders had for years, in pursuance of personal power and ambition, resorted to misrepresentation, manipulation and a hidden agenda. It took the form of a personal fight with anyone who operated within the capitalist system, and, of course, in the front line were the employers and that meant the managers.

I started to speak to larger groups of workers and this extension of my activities showed up an embarrassing weakness or flaw in my ability. I had a phobia that caused me to suffer what I can only describe as stage fright. Try as hard as I could, on many occasions, and actually speaking at large gatherings, my attempts always resulted in anything but a good speech. I resolved to be brief and to stay on course with the pen as a means of transmitting my thoughts, leaving others to do the rest. The fact that I was invariably voicing a minority opinion in the presence of a hostile audience might have excused me to a degree, but in reality, I should have been able to master the problem. There was no doubt about it, there was a desperate need for something to be done.

One of my early efforts, (before ORMO-TU started) was a letter I wrote to the Oxford Mail, published on Friday 4 February 1972, in which I supported the idea (at the time of the miners strike) that it was unnecessary for the car factory workers to strike in support of the miners, who historically have wielded more power on their own than any other group of workers. There was a good deal of moral blackmail exercised at the time of the miners' dispute. They could have considered Cowley Assembly exempt from supporting their strike on the grounds that we were constantly losing money, fighting battles of our own. I don't think it occurred to our people to ask the miners to strike and close down a couple mines in support of the car workers when we were having problems. Perhaps that is what we should have done.

I wrote two more letters to the Oxford Mail in 1972. One was published on 22 April and the other on the 20 October. The April one expressed approval at the way the Assembly Plant employees had settled their pay negotiations without striking, while at the neighbouring Body Plant, their dispute had caused us to lose two weeks pay because, as always, their failure to supply our factory with car bodies stopped us as well. The Body Plant workers cancelled out our peaceful settlement.

The October letter was headlined '*End Cowley Stoppages*' and went as follows: '*In recent days we have had stoppages, planned and abandoned mass meetings and management instructed shut-downs, sometimes with three or four different issues all being pursued at once. The resulting loss of pay, company revenue, customer goodwill and working men's credibility does nothing but harm. To begin with, the need not only to think 'Don't Strike but to think Anti-Strike', is the order of the day. Evidence that the anti-strike mood already exists has been demonstrated several times recently, notably by the night shift, over the mix-up when the senior shop steward decided to proceed with a one day token strike on 28 August against the wishes of a 2000 majority. Even here, the thinking went wrong because a stoppage took place to protest about a decision to strike. Stopping work to protest at the wayward activities of elected representatives is surely self-defeating. Far better to stick doggedly to one's job and conduct the protest passively and keep conspicuously in the right. It will take patience and determination because in some cases a minority will still leave their jobs and earnings will cease, but at least the activists would be separated from the anti-activists and a clear picture emerge. What is needed is a cool determination not to strike (official strikes being the exception) and to relentlessly search for alternative means of persuading employers to concede, at least in part, the demands being made. I believe that a leadership that advocated such a policy, and got it working would have such an advantage over the others that it would be able to wring practically anything out of the management. They, as well as the workers are bitter and sick of the present internal set-up and would bend over backwards to allow the work people to have more than what they are getting, to support an arrangement that was less destructive to the industry. What was frightening, was the ability of a minority to exert pressure on the management on issues that have little or no merit.*' The letter ended, '*I do not think that British Leyland will ever cease activities here, but I am sure we shall miss the best opportunities if we don't sort ourselves out very soon.*'

CHAPTER THREE

Get in the Queue

> *A queue in dispatch, I nearly blot my copybook.*
> *The Directors get it wrong.*
> *The costly die is cast.*

'Since 1973 the car industry in Oxford was more or less in permanent decline, linked as it was to the fortunes of what, by the late 1960s, had become Oxford's only motor manufacturing employer of any size. The British Leyland Motor Corporation, - BLMC - was formed following a merger between Leyland Motor Corporation and British Motor Holdings, in 1968. The merger unified all of the major independents still operating in British car manufacture at that time. That was Rover, Austin Morris, Jaguar and Triumph. It created a vast and, some people said, unwieldy empire employing about 198,000 people world-wide and selling more than a million vehicles a year.'
(See acknowledgement section, Ref. Lord McCarthy's *The Future of Cowley*, enquiry report)

On one occasion information filtered through that a stoppage of work had taken place in the paint rectification section, in the Dispatch department. The problem was to do with payments. While that strike by the painters was holding up production, another two groups, namely the inspectors and the production car drivers also went into dispute. The procedure for dealing with a new dispute involving strike action is, for an industrial relations officer to contact the senior shop stewards office and tell them to get someone to the location of the dispute as soon as possible. In this particular case, as the senior stewards of all three unions were engaged in discussions with the management on the painters' dispute, deputy seniors were dispatched to contact the inspectors and drivers representatives. On arrival, the inspectors' and drivers' stewards said they were in dispute about payments and they were anxious to join the painters' strike. It was pointed out to them that, as production had already been stopped, the maximum pressure had already been applied, and for their members to join the strike now was unnecessary. The time for them to strike was when the painters had got what they wanted and production had restarted. In effect, the advice given to the drivers and the inspectors was 'get in the queue'.

When I heard about this, as a shop steward, I nearly blotted my copybook in the presence of some of my department members. Without thinking, I said that if the management give in to them (meaning the strikers) on this issue, they needed their heads examined. Fortunately, those present showed no reaction to my statement, which could have been interpreted as supporting the management when what I was doing was trying to discourage 'wildcat' strikes, (unofficial, instant walk outs) which were destined to become the scourge of the industry for many years ahead. However, my members seemed not to notice and said nothing.

It was customary for the management to be contacted by Head Office, to give a daily report on the current production programme. When told that a stoppage of production due to a dispute was holding things up, adding that the industrial relations officers had been told to make a stand and not to concede to the strikers' demands, Head Office ended the discussion by instructing the plant management to 'keep the factory running'. It left the industrial relations officers with no bargaining power and they had to go back to the senior stewards and give them what they wanted. Head Office had snatched the rug from under the feet of the whole industrial relations department, by taking the soft option.

From then on, when any group of workers, large or small, were putting their grievance to the senior stewards, the seniors would say 'You know what you have to do, get out on the road' (unofficial meetings were not allowed on company premises, 'the road' was outside the factory gates). From then on, those senior, deputy senior and leading shop stewards became the most ruthless leaders ever to hold office, at the Assembly Plant.

If the person at headquarters had supported the local management, instead of washing their hands of the matter, and been prepared to explain to all of the employees, factory wide, why they were not going to engage in piecemeal bargaining arrangements, and then let the trade union leaders wait, and the factory stay at a standstill until they realised that the management meant what they said, a few lessons like that, would have saved years of disruption, wasted investment, lost industries and avoided the UK from having a reputation for being strike happy, disruptive and wrong. Perhaps, as an added bonus, there would have been no need, ten years later, for the services of Margaret (later, Lady) Thatcher.

CHAPTER FOUR

Chuck Him Out!

> *The conduct of the Joint Shop Stewards Committee meetings.*
> *The freedom to speak.* • *'Chuck him out' they said.*
> *I was recruited to become more active by a reliable 'old timer'.*

'Until the mid 1970s, employment, sales and profits remained relatively stable. But the combined effects of the first 'oil shock' of 1973, the growing import penetration of the UK market and - linked to this - the rapid growth of international competition in the car industry, laid bare fundamental weaknesses in British Leyland Motor Corporation's position. A failure to invest adequately, which was evident in the ageing model range, forced the Company into crisis in 1975. That year the Company teetered on the edge of collapse. Although the losses sustained were relatively modest, the particular set of circumstances facing the Company at that time meant that bankruptcy became a real possibility'
(See acknowledgement section, Ref. Lord McCarthy's *The Future of Cowley*, enquiry report)

In 1968, when told that I had won the election to be a shop steward, I resolved to carry out my new responsibilities positively and energetically, Besides the daily casework, and administrative activities, membership card checks, communications etc. there was a programme of regular meetings.

My union Branch	fortnightly own time
My union Shop Stewards Committee,	monthly own time
My union District Committee	own time
The factory Joint Shop Stewards Committee	own time
Management approved Joint Shop Stewards Committee	paid, in working hours
Works Consultative Production Committee	paid, in working hours
The Company Suggestion Committee	paid, in working hours
The Corporation Quality & Reliability Campaign weekly	paid, in working hours
Oxford Trades Union Council (the local TUC)	monthly own time
I attended protest marches in London.	lose a days pay
I attended protest marches in Oxford.	own time, Saturday
I was also an active member of the Labour Party.	

The casework in the factory, otherwise known as union business, meant leaving my workshop bay and running around, with or without management permission or knowledge. The Joint Shop Stewards Committee was the powerhouse of the unions at the factory. The practical arrangements for calling together two hundred and fifty stewards to a meeting would mean stopping production. That number of operatives was too great to be replaced by relief workers and spare labour. It was usually expected by management that the union leaders (senior shop stewards of both unions) would limit the duration of the meeting to one hour. It was also usual for that period of time to be exceeded, sometimes doubled. One of the first statements to be made by the chairman, on opening the meeting, would be to announce that everyone present would be paid at their full rate. That put the members in an appreciative frame of mind towards the leaders, for having negotiated such terms.

The employers would be seeking to obtain the agreement for more effort from the workers or a change of practices that perhaps didn't require more effort but had a disturbance factor, such as an increased night-work requirement. The urgency justified the costly loss of production, while the shop stewards made their way to the meeting, attended at the meeting and made their way back to their individual work stations after the meeting.

The managements initiative would be accompanied by the hint that they were actively considering imposition of their requirement, and a showdown, should a failure to agree be the outcome of the meeting.

Just the stuff union leaders are used to. The ultra militant and revolutionaries relish yet another opportunity to flex their industrial muscle, another chance to strike a blow at the company's finances. Part of the agreement to pay the two hundred and fifty shop stewards while at the meeting, was that the senior stewards would spell out the seriousness of the occasion and, at the very least, they would not advocate or propose a strike.

Having explained the details of the discussions with management, to the meeting, the shop stewards are given an opportunity to respond. Up go a few hands, the chairman recognises most of the people who want to speak and could predict what each one will say. Fighting talk! The first to speak starts.

'*We have to make a stand, my members are adamant they won't accept the management's proposals*'. Another member speaks. '*It's another turn of the screw, how many more times are they going to come at us like this, the job won't be worth a light the way things are going. We have to stop it here and now. Strikes are the only thing management take notice* of. A third member with his hand up starts to speak. '*I agree with the last two speakers. My members are at rock bottom, Morale among my men and women are at an all time low and who can blame them. On tele last night I see the Germans are getting nearly twice as much as us for doing the same job*'. The fourth member to have his hand up is me. '*I consulted my members and I have to say, they will not strike unless and until it's made official*'. I am in a tiny minority again. There was a groan all round, muted insults. I am unabashed amongst the activists. I almost enjoy it. Sometimes one or two people who speak will water down the criticism and say there is some merit in what Gatehouse says, it didn't make any difference to the decision of the meeting. The vote was put and decision taken, they will strike.

It was at this stage, that I was recruited by the late Les Davies, who was the secretary of the Works Production Consultative Committee, an elderly man whose early industrial experience was in Hartlepool Docks unloading ships. In those days he often represented workers who were less articulate, at means tested tribunals, that was in the early 1930's depression. He persuaded me to 'get yourself onto the production Committee' and while I was about it 'to start attending my union branch meetings on a regular basis, to support him and one or two others in an attempt to stop the communists gaining control, which prompted me to start a twenty-two year stint of regular attendance, all to no avail, they took office and promptly voted in a committed communist supporter as the new chairman. I was mostly in a minority at shop stewards and branch meetings, but consoled myself, safe in the knowledge that the vast majority of ordinary non-active members wanted nothing to do with communism.

I have referred to the Joint Shop Stewards Committee as high powered, and in my early days as a shop steward it was a bit nerve racking for me to attend, especially when the purpose of the meeting was to call a major strike on an important issue. At these times I knew it was likely to get unanimous support from the shop stewards present, and I was going to be almost totally alone when making any statement in opposition to the call for a strike. I used to stride up and down, racking my brain trying to find a sound basis for an argument against a strike, and in the very early days displayed a fair bit of emotional stress when speaking to what was a hugely hostile gathering. After a few such meetings I gradually got to grips with the problem and my confidence grew sufficiently for me to continue, while still holding to my minority belief, that excessive militancy was counter productive, and was destroying our livelihood. Regrettably, it took years for that to sink in.

My method of operating was to apply Satrene's rules of debate, and that meant raising 'points of order' to break into the debate and so either challenge a statement or put a different point of view. This was very effective because invariably there were one or two people who would back me up. Often it would start a split and then there might be an appeal to have me thrown out of the meeting. To be fair, when Bob Fryer was the chairman, he would say I had a right to be there, to represent my members, and it was up to them to deal with it and, in any case, the meeting could ignore what I said. I did this for years and was well known for my 'points of order'.

On one occasion I attended a meeting well aware that I had recently upset the militants in a big way. Everyone had sat down. The senior steward took up his position on the platform and was about to open the meeting when someone from the floor stood up and spoke. '*Excuse me chairman, before you open the meeting, I have to tell you that my members have told me, that if Roy*

Gatehouse was at this meeting I, and the other stewards in our department were to leave the meeting.' The chairman, Bob Fryer, said that Gatehouse had a right to be there, and that was that, so a group of stewards started to leave the meeting. Up pops another steward and says he and the other stewards in his department were in the same position, and they started to leave, and yet a third steward stood up to do the same. At this point I turned round and said to a steward by the name of Cliff Moss who was sat in the row behind, *'If I thought that I was not wanted at this meeting, I would leave'*. Needless to say, I stayed, and, incidentally, so did the protesting stewards. To this day, I am astonished at what I was allowed to get away with. Some while later, Bob Fryer and I met in the works canteen. We were walking in opposite directions and as he approached, he said to me *' You stabbed me in the back'*, and I said *'I did not stab you in the back Bob, I stabbed you in the front'*, and we both kept walking.

Meanwhile, my friend Michael Denver, whose idea it was to start up ORMO-TU said he was concerned about the very real threat that revolutionary militancy, as advocated by the activities of Alan Thornett and his supporters, was still an issue. A leaflet had just been handed out with the usual clap-trap, plus an invitation to attend one of their public meetings. Mick announced that he intended to go. As usual it was to be held at the Cowley Community Centre.

I liked the idea and was interested in the outcome and his account of what had taken place. Sure enough, a couple of days later Mick related to me what had happened. He said he located the room, went in and sat on one of the chairs that had been set out in rows, a bit like a small classroom. He noted there were twenty chairs available with a table and two more chairs set out for the chairman and the speaker. By the time the meeting was due to start, one more chair had to be found, presumably because the usual twenty plus a member of the public had turned up. We found the whole thing highly amusing, especially the propaganda.

A short time later I decided to attend one of these meetings, and when my wife heard where I was going, it being a pleasant summer evening, decided to accompany me. We got to the venue a little early, made our way to the meeting room and were immediately conscious that our attendance had caused a stir amongst those already there. They stood around chatting and one of them would pop out to greet each new arrival with, *'Gatehouse is here, he's in there now'*. Of course they needed two more chairs.

Eventually, in breezed Thornett, carrying the most crammed brief case I have ever seen, accompanied by the chairman. He made his way to the table, plonked the paperwork down and said *'I am not opening this meeting while Gatehouse is here, he is a management spy and he's been rattling around the factory for five years.'* I stood up and said *'Alan this is a public meeting and I am entitled to be here.'* Thornett said *'Get out'*. A couple of young males went over to the exit door, presenting to my mind a physical presence and perhaps a threat. I started to leave and to my surprise Barbara, my wife made no move.

She was going to stay. *'Come on love'*, I said, and indicated that I wanted her to leave. She grudgingly went ahead of me, giving me the distinct feeling that I had robbed her of an interesting experience. As we left, the last thing I said, for the benefit of the other people at the meeting, was *'I am just an independent minded person, that is all'*. I was quite happy with what had happened. I had a witness to the event. Thornett had displayed fear of a challenge and had acted undemocratically and I was in a position to call the shots. My first decision was to tell no-one, not even my friend Michael Denver.

The day after the meeting was a Friday, the 6 September 1974, and an ordinary working day. I went to work as usual and was comfortable with regard to the previous day's events. There was no reaction. The following Monday was the same and it was not until Thursday that stories started to circulate. Thornett was boasting that he had thrown me out of his meeting. I was happy with the distinction he had bestowed upon me. There was no adverse reaction and I basked in a bit of factory wide publicity.

CHAPTER FIVE

Meetings

*A slightly 'hypothetical' mass meeting. • I vote to strike.
National Publicity. • The bosses fight back.
Another mass meeting. • National union officers intervene.*

The hold some union leaders have over their members must be mystifying to outsiders. Workers get labelled 'mindless morons who follow their leaders like sheep'. This is an over simplification of the facts. Votes by a show of hands are taken, often after a loaded and biased process of communication has been executed. Circumstances vary from one mass meeting to another, but in the early stages of a dispute, issues are clear cut.

For instance on one occasion, the workers were called together in their thousands, to decide what course of action to take, in support of their claim, in their 'Pay and Working Conditions Annual Review'. All avenues of agreement had been explored, between the management up to Plant Director level, and the union's senior shop stewards, but to no avail, no agreement had been reached, there is no option but a trial of strength. The management in those circumstances introduced measures to minimise the effect of an open ended strike, and the union leaders set about cultivating support from their members. Regular union branch meetings, had been kept up to date with the negotiations, albeit attended by only 2% of the membership, a motion was adopted that said 'This branch calls upon the senior stewards to recommend strike action at any mass meeting, called for the purpose of deciding a course of action in pursuit of more pay and specified improvements in working conditions'. The clear-cut scenario.

At the first mass meeting, the leaders of both unions addressed those present, a report was given on the discussions with management, the terms offered explained, and the need for positive support from all those present, spelt out. The senior stewards, stressed that improvements in the company's offer, was there for those who were prepared to fight.

The senior stewards conformed to the resolution from the T. & G.W.U. Branch and called for a show of hands. 'Those in favour of strike action to improve the Company's offer, please show'. I am at this meeting and my hand goes up with all the others. Over whelming support, almost unanimous, 'Hands down' those against strike action please show'. Half a dozen brave people put their hands up and a smile spreads across the faces of those on the platform, they are no threat, and magnanimity towards those scattered dissenters costs nothing. The resolution was passed and the 'seniors' had then got something they could get their teeth into.

Because the meeting had been held on a Friday morning, the night shift workers had an opportunity to attend, though in truth, very few did so, because the decision to support the call for a strike was totally predictable, and they were keen to get home, get some sleep, then to start their long weekend off. (They were not due back until the following Monday evening.)

On the first Thursday after the strike started, the workers all returned to the factory, in the afternoon, to collect their pay. They were all milling around, their cars clogging the local streets in the factory area, those that didn't bother to put them in the company car park.

Some cars had their families with them, ready to shoot-off straight to the supermarket to get the weeks shopping, they waited in the car expecting the wage earner to quickly nip to their pay station, collect their money and nip back, but their return was delayed, because having collected their pay, they had searched around for their shop steward, or supervisor, anyone who might be able to tell them of any development in the dispute. What was happening, how were the negotiations going? When was the next mass meeting to be held? More in hope than expectation. Past experience told them it will be at least another week, probably two, before one side or the other shows signs of a willingness to talk. Cowley factory workers are paid one week in hand, that means that although they had been on strike for a week, they still had one week's pay to come. They can pay their bills this week but next week, who knows? That is why they were eager to find out when they can start earning again. On their terms of course. The workers were then out of touch with the employers and their shop stewards. Collectively, they only met while at work. Being home with no money coming in, was uncomfortable, knowing from experience that shop stewards in general, and senior stewards in particular, were always reluctant to even consider ending a strike. The union leaders were heading for a situation where they were not only being pressured to return to work by the employers, from then on there was also the growing tendency for their members to want to get back to work.

Of course, the strikers are not only fellow workers but are also neighbours in the community, at such times they and their spouses discuss the situation over the garden fence or at the bus stop, wherever they meet idle workers tend to indulge in philosophising on the unfairness of it all, and recall the statement made by the senior steward who addressed the meeting, when he said 'there was an improvement in the company's offer, for those prepared to fight'.

One bloke told me he had seen a senior shop steward doing a window cleaning job and he showed me a snap shot of the person 'on location' as it were. His point being, was he 'digging in' for a long, debilitating strike? As for the snap shot, I expressed my shock, bordering on alarm at the possible consequences for himself, if the senior steward in question found out about the flagrant intrusion of his privacy. Anyway, when I advised him to dispose of the snap, he didn't seem to understand what all the fuss was about. That situation was likely to produce something stronger than a polite request to hand over the offending film and photos.

The local media (Oxford Mail) publicise their calculations on how much the strike was costing the company in terms of cars lost at showroom prices. Which puts it in millions of pounds within the first few days. This affects the attitude of local outsiders towards the workers and the trade unions. It is a blatant exaggeration because showroom prices include the car purchase tax, delivery and number plate fees, road fund licence and even a tank full of fuel. They also gave space to anyone that advocated an early settlement, and the moderates (me included) started to count and recall the number of occasions when strikes had taken place with dire consequences in lost earnings. Some of them, when small groups gained settlements at the expense of the majority who were not on strike, but were shut out without pay.

The national newspapers put brief reports at the foot of their front page, or tucked away somewhere else, without comment at that stage. The T. & G.W.U. were the controlling force at the factory, and a dominant faction within that union, in pursuit of their obsession for uncompromising militancy, meant the chances of the dispute moving towards a settlement were minimal, partly because an (unofficial) negotiating committee, were lobbying the senior stewards and the full time, union officials, every time they stepped outside the conference room, vociferously opposing any chance of a compromise solution offered by management. At best and in desperation, the company offered to recall the work force, and to sanction a paid mass meeting, if the senior stewards on the platform, calling for a vote, would undertake not to recommend rejection of the company's offer. The union side agreed to consider the matter.

Another week goes by and things were starting to happen. Information leaked out that the management had spoken to the local press and revealed that they had sent letters to all of the employee's homes, and in those letters they set out their position and urged them to accept their offer of an increase in pay, plus the implementation of most of the points on conditions their representatives had demanded.

The unions were furious, claiming that the company had 'gone behind their backs' by writing to their members. They demanded the meeting be unconditional and be a paid mass meeting, of all the strikers, and when the company activates the recall, the <u>unions</u> would notify the local press.

Management recall letters were sent on the Monday morning on the beginning of the third week of the strike. They had further discussions with the unions over the weekend in a hotel on the outskirts of Oxford. The letters stated it was to be a paid meeting, gave the time of the day shift workers meeting, as 7.15a.m. Wednesday and the location, at 'The Barracks sports ground'. The night shift meeting was at 8pm. on the Wednesday and the location was 'in the factory'.

Wednesday. 7.15am. On the sports ground. The workers had gathered in their thousands, the person from High Wycombe who was contracted by the unions to provide the amplified speaker system had set it up and disappeared, Gargy Patel from Radio Oxford was present in her usual unobtrusive style, also the late Peter Sturges, reporting for the Oxford Mail. The masses of workers impatiently wanting to know whether they would be going back to work, out of necessity rather than desire, or whether they were going to be talked into staying out on strike.

'Good morning Brothers and sisters' it was Bob Fryer the senior steward for the T. & G.W.U. speaking in that familiar mixture of East European and broken English accent of his, it was no wonder he did most of the speaking from the platform, he never needed notes, he had it all at his fingertips. He was still angry, over the actions of the management when they had notified the press of their decision to send letters to the strikers. Underhanded and provocative was the way the unions saw it. The gist of what he had to say was that the company had not done enough to satisfy the unions claim, especially on the pay rise, and the negotiating team recommended that the strike should continue. This brought about a groan from the members. The next speaker was a senior steward representing the A.U.E W., the Engineers Union. He justified the claim they had submitted by comparing it with other groups of workers who were getting more for doing the same work and also compared it with what some of the bosses get, for doing next to nothing.

The most telling point was made when a resolution from the most militant branch of the T. & G.W.U. was read out by Bob Fryer, it said 'That this branch calls upon the Senior Stewards to recommend that the strike continues until the claim has been met in full' There was an immediate reaction from groups of workers in the crowd. 'No' they shouted, there was a pause, and then the shouting started again and began to involve more and more people, The leaders on the platform appeared to be arguing about what to do next, a deputy senior steward who was a member of the branch that had sent the resolution moved up to the platform and could be seen talking to Bob Fryer, who was bent down listening, and when he had finished Bob took the microphone and called for order in the crowd. When they had quietened down Bob said, 'first of all, it is quite within rule to take a motion from the branch and if some of you don't like it, you are going to get a chance to vote on it in a minute, so don't worry'. The point is that although we are not operating in a corporate bargaining situation, I have just been told that Longbridge (another British Leyland factory in Birmingham) are about now, taking the same decision as us on a similar claim, and are confident that there will, by a massive majority vote to continue their strike, now whether that is the case or not, I don't know'.

Bob Fryer starts to talk again, 'Now I am going to put the vote again. It is 'that we continue with the strike until our demands are met in full, please show', up go the hands, there seems to be some confusion, a minority raise their hands, 'do you understand the resolution?', Bob asks. 'Those in favour of staying on strike until the company have met our claim in full, please show', very little response again, the hands that were up, start to drop. Clearly the motion is lost 'O.K that motion is lost is has been suggested that another motion be put, 'that the strike continue until the cash offer is significantly improved, and bear in mind the position we shall be in, if Longbridge succeed in securing more than us, O.K. then. Those in favour please show' says Bob, the hands went up in greater numbers, but still with a large number all over the park abstaining, and obviously confused. The people on the platform systematically scanned the crowd, 'come on, come on, keep them up, O.K. hands down', 'those against continuing the strike, please show,' it's close, another minority, it was now obvious that there were massive abstentions. 'The motion is carried' says Bob, 'no' roar a small group in the crowd. There was confusion on the platform, two or three were talking to Bob at once, one person jumped from the platform, followed by another. There is shouting from the crowd, and the remainder leave the platform, no one had formally closed the meeting. The decision stood as far as the leaders were concerned, the strike was still on. The workers drifted away, mostly back to the factory to see where the management stood on the issue. After a while the supervision were told tell their people to go home and to await recall notices via the usual channels.

The night shift meeting, such as it was, voted to return to work and were told by the management the same as the day shift, to go home until they were recalled. The next day it was reported in most of the newspapers that the British Leyland factory workers at Longbridge had voted to accept the companies pay and conditions settlement and were back at work, while at Cowley, Oxford, a spokes person for the unions told the Press that Cowley day shift had voted to stay on strike, but the night shift had voted to accept the company's offer, adding that none of the Cowley car workers were back at work.

The dispute ended as so many did at Cowley, in utter chaos. The employers called in the national officers of both unions, who spelt out slightly revised terms and said the company claimed, that the investment programme, precluded any more money being on offer for the current round of wage increases, but would provide the basis for the company and the employee's future prosperity,

The national union officers notified the local officials that the end of the road had been reached, as far as negotiations were concerned, and the members should return to work.

CHAPTER SIX
Trotsky's

> *A friend attends a Trotsky meeting.*
> *Barbara and I attend a Trotsky meeting, Thornett boasts,*
> *'we threw him out'.*
> *Surepticious behaviour at branch meetings.*
> *My union national officer visits Oxford.*

In the 6th Edition of ORMO, dated October 1973, we urged members to attend their union branch meetings occasionally and explained to them what to expect and how to deal with it. The final point we made on that subject was to point out that they would be unlikely to see their shop steward in attendance because all too often they are happy to act as stewards while they are being paid at work, but duck out when it comes to giving up their own time. The glaring exception to that is the example of the militants (especially the revolutionaries), but, generally speaking, they are the activists, and at Cowley they called the shots.

Initially, my branch meetings were reasonably friendly, and, bearing in mind that I was outspoken in an 'opposite point of view' way, I got used to being excluded from some confidentialities, but did not mind that in the least. On one occasion, I detected conspiratorial tones which aroused my curiosity, and gleaned the fact that Brother Hugh Scanlon (see page 56), the National President of our union was to address a meeting of the faithful in St. Michaels Hall in Oxford. The surreptitious behaviour was about selection and exclusion, spreading the word to the selected members and exclusion of the non-believers (in this case, the Right Wingers or Moderates). It worked thus. Scanlon believed in working towards socialism, so did the communists, so did 'Engineering Voice' Oxford Committee, and they didn't want moderates asking awkward questions at public meetings.

However, I was there and provocatively sat next to the Oxford Mail reporter who must have been standing in for (the late) Peter Sturges, their regular industrial correspondent. I say provocatively because I was told by one of the branch elders that it was not the done thing to be cosying-up to the capitalist press. Anyway, for the benefit of the new correspondent, I voluntarily identified by name the people he might want to quote. I was quoted in the Oxford Mail thus, sub-titled 'Harming ourselves'. *He (Brother Scanlon) was answering a question from an Austin Morris shop steward, Mr Roy Gatehouse, who said, 'We have now got a situation where I can't see us getting a full week's work and the people doing us most harm are our fellow workers.*

The only answer is for some form of co-ordination, which means restriction. This problem is now on everyone's lips. We have to have some sort of policy on getting together and not destroying ourselves'. I was pleased with the fruits of my intervention, not to mention the publicity!

Branch meetings, as one would expect, were the one vital access point where the ordinary union member could participate in union activity, usually to seek advice of some kind, or to chase some entitlement, but, more often than not, in response to an active member trying to recruit new activists for the purpose of promoting militancy. There is nothing wrong with that.

The structure of the AEU (Amalgamated Engineering Union), as it was then known, in the Oxford area consisted of twelve branches, nine of which were within Oxford city limits, the remainder in the surrounding towns. Branches were represented on Oxford District Committee by an elected delegate, though in some cases one person represented two (paired) branches. When the branch I was in was taken over by Communists and their supporters, they elected a member of the Communist Party into the position of chairman, and he was also elected as the branch delegate to the District Committee. All of this activity took place during my early days as a shop steward and I had much to learn, particularly in regard to dealing with, what was after all, an established national political party. The British Communist Party was run and supported by able people, including middle class academics, not that I was particularly conscious of that at the time, but they were not to be treated as fools.

When I started taking them to task, and with my habit of putting things into print, I was warned by the branch chairman that *up North someone had been prosecuted for describing another person as a Communist, when in fact it could not be proved.* That frightened the life out of me and for quite some time I studiously avoided doing just that, and resorted to using the phrase 'excessively militant'. This was an example of the battle of wits that was part of branch life, while struggling to exercise an influence.

Another ploy at branch meetings was to tell newcomers and non regulars, that it was against union rules for individuals to issue any document at election time, naming alternative candidates to those nominated by the branch, The tactic was for the branch regulars to nominate and select the candidate of their choice, when only the small group of activists are present and then as the election campaign built up and the non activists started to respond by turning out to vote, they would be told that they had to support the official branch nominee. This repressive policy was typical of how communists fought to exclude the mass of ordinary members from exercising choice at elections. I still have two tickets that were handed to me, by a party member, naming the communist nominated, candidates, but not the ticket-issuing organisation. We at ORMO-TU published the names of our candidates in our regular leaflets, and I was cautioned by the District Secretary, but I knew too much for him to make a formal complaint.

The militants were always against rules that were introduced to promote democracy, for instance, for the election of full time union officers, instead of the elections taking place at branch meetings where only a tiny minority of members attended. The rules were changed. The new rule said all such ballots had to be carried out by post, the ballot papers to be sent to the member's home address, filled in and returned by post to the Electoral Reform Society. The militants campaigned against it. ORMO-TU campaigned in support of these changes, and won, because we knew, not only would more members take part, but those that did vote would be able to exercise their judgement without interference from anyone. What we were doing, was policing branch meetings, by exposing their undemocratic manoeuvres. When unable to out-vote them, then publicise their activities

There was the proposed change of rule, to allow the employers to deduct subscriptions from workers pay packets and transfer them to the appropriate union. It was more convenient for the union members, and more efficient for the unions. It was advantageous to everyone involved. The militants did not like it. They fought tooth and nail, and lost! The pro-democracy rule changes were voted in by the masses of ordinary workers who did not like the antics of the excessively militant, when they were in control.

Another strange practice of the communists, when at union meetings, was to predict the total collapse of the world capitalist financial system, they would say so in the most confident manner. It was always a mystery to me but I never lost any sleep over it.

ORMO-TU 7th Edition, October 1973 headlined. *'Leaflet Handouts on the Factory Gates'* and went on as follows. *'There are now something like eight unofficial organisations handing out publications to the factory employees, all on the subject of politics and/or the trade unions, ORMO-TU is included in this count. This leaflet has the distinction of being the only one that makes a bid for peace. Less unofficial strikes was our constant theme, not necessarily no unofficial strikes - we know the value of controlled stoppages. To adopt this policy would bring instant profit, as the loss of wages would be reduced. We who produce ORMO-TU think it has another distinction, that it represents the views of the majority of the workforce at the Assembly Plant. Our readers are invited to form their own opinions on how right we are.'*

The leaflet ended with a statement relating to ORMO-TU finances. Abbreviated, it read, 'three hundred subscriptions so far - balance £15.87'.

The 8th Edition of ORMO, distributed in November 1973, said, *'A More Honest View of a Problem. We challenge the claim by the militants that people are leaving the Assembly Plant for jobs outside because the rates of pay at the factory have been overtaken by wage levels elsewhere. Everyone who comes to work at the factory knows in advance how much they will be paid if they work a full week. Secondly, if the pattern of departures is studied it will be noticed that more people leave at the time of major disputes or soon after, than at times of more continuous working. Thirdly, more people leave the South side, where there has been more stoppages, than the North side, and finally, it disregards a senior steward's statement in the T&GWU 5/55 Branch News earlier this year, 'that wages and conditions are second to none'.'*

A constantly changing membership is not in our interests, unity and strength comes with a stable workforce with people who have a long-term interest in secure employment. Thought should be given to people who were enticed away from jobs they had held for many years and to whom £46.20 per week would have meant an improvement in their circumstances. It is not difficult to imagine their disappointment when they found their average earnings at the factory work out at something like £34.00 per week (because of strikes etc), and they realise that potentially substantial redundancy payments from companies they left had been sacrificed on an unsuccessful attempt to try factory life.

CHAPTER SEVEN

Elections

> *Elected as delegate to represent two union branches on Oxford District Committee.*
> *I ask 'where the hell are we going District Secretary'?*

In 1975 I decided to stand in the elections as the delegate for two branches on the Oxford District Committee, of the AUEW. Having got myself nominated, my name appeared on the ballot papers together with that of Michael (Mick) Soanes, the incumbent candidate.

ORMO-TU had been launched and distributed for two years, and had given me widespread publicity within the factory, It enhanced my chance of success come election time.

The following is a verbatim copy of the letter sent to my branch secretary, from Oxford District Secretary, giving the results of the election. (see page 28)

Branch voting returns:	Cowley 203 CE	Oxford No. 2
Gatehouse R	46	13
Soanes M.J.	35	8

As for the return sheet received from Cowley 203CE (which was my branch) shows one more vote was cast than the number of signatures on the recording sheet. I, as returning officer, have therefore declared invalid the votes cast in Cowley 203 CE branch. Brother R. Gatehouse is therefore declared elected as district committee man by 13 votes to 8, with Brother M. J. Soanes as Provisional Representative.

M.W. Young (bearing his signature)
District Secretary

Malcolm Young the Engineering union District Secretary, and David Buckle the Transport and General Workers, District Secretary were as different as chalk and cheese. David had a high profile in the community, in the City of Oxford, and as a County Councillor for Oxfordshire, and of course, in the trade union movement. He was outgoing and open minded, enjoyed prolonged service as a trade union leader, was a magistrate (chaired the local Bench), was on the board of directors at The Oxford Play House theatre, and involved in a myriad of other activities. In contrast, Malcolm Young who also had a prolonged service but was known mainly by the skilled workers whose numbers were shrinking by hundreds, if not thousands and older workers who were retiring. Malcolm was less open about his political preferences, which can and did effect his position while acting as a trade union representative.

From the late 1950s through to the 1980s, the growth in union membership due to the Closed Shop agreement, meant membership of a recognised union was compulsory, the T&GWU in the Cowley Car factories had multiplied its numbers time and time again, while the membership of the AUEW declined, in a big way.

In the latter years, at the Assembly Plant (where I worked) the method of recruiting new union members was carried out at the induction of new employees. The group of new workers would be assembled in a conference room and would be addressed by an AUEW senior steward whose job it was to persuade as many of them as possible to join his union, then a T&GWU senior steward, who always offered better services, persuaded the vast majority to join the T&GWU which lead to a further decline, and influence of AUEW.

On one occasion, I rang district office and spoke to Malcolm about the situation at the factory. True to form, chaos reigned. Small and large groups of workers all over the factory had stopped work and were in dispute. It was worrying and I felt apprehensive about it. I telephoned district office and when he came on the line I asked him my usual question at such times. 'Where the hell are we going, Malcolm', and all he could say was 'I think the workforce up there are strike weary'. There was no, 'leave it with me, I'll see if there is anything I can do about it'. He seemed totally unconcerned. At the time, that made me angry, and I am still angry. Here was a chance for him to call in the AUEW senior shop steward at the factory, a man by the name of Doug Hobbs, (deceased) and instruct him to distance our union from all of the unofficial 'wild cat' type of strikes, that were damaging the workers finances as much as it was the company's. In other words to tell Doug Hobbs what he should do, instead of allowing the leaders of the T&GWU to do so.

In fact, he could have grabbed the initiative and defended the ordinary workers who were being manipulated into causing industrial chaos, and, the unstoppable reprisals by the employers. More than that, he could have retrieved some respect for our union at the factory that had been lost through years of weak leadership. But no, he, Malcolm, chose to leave it to David Buckle, who eventually consolidated his position as a realist by enlisting the services of the T&GWU senior shop steward at the factory, Reg Parsons, who was the only man who was prepared to make a stand against those who were the cause of the disruption.

If I could address the Communists, the Marxists and the Trotskyist for one moment, I want to tell them that Malcolm, to the best of my knowledge, never stood in their way, I would expect him to pride himself, on being able to say, quite truthfully, that he never went against anyone who supported the workers struggle to get more out of life than they are offered under capitalism

I recall two more incidents, both identify speakers invited by Malcolm to the AUEW quarterly shop stewards meeting at the Oxford Town Hall, One was the Distribution Manager of the Morning Star which is the daily newspaper published for the British Communist Party, and the other was a national officer in the engineering union, who later became a Labour MP in a London constituency. In his own brief introduction proudly claimed that in his early days as an activist he was thrown out of twenty six jobs in eighteen months. To me that spoke volumes, it was the most telling statement of his talk. Do I need to ask the question, what good was he to the people he was representing when his time with them was so short, or had he got some way of negotiating with the employers after they had sacked him?

CHAPTER EIGHT
Shop Stewards

> *About shop stewards.*
> *How it is supposed to work?* • *The employers involvement.*
> *How representative are the union leaders?*

Trade union activists, in the main, are people who are concerned about the amount of power the employers have over their employees and the difficulties the employees experience as a result. The employees concern is translated into organised collective resistance to the employers demands, until they have seen that their interests, in the form of financial reward, safety and the general burden is reasonable. An honourable objective if carried out honourably. In reality the trade union activists range politically from a shop steward who always votes Conservative, to a revolutionary who openly uses his/her considerable influence to advocate and practice radical policies.

Shop stewards are the first level of representation and authority in the trade union movement, collectively and with clever leadership, they are as powerful as employers allow them to be. For a long period of time the management at Cowley, lost control. Anarchy reigned, until they appealed to the National officers of the unions, to intervene and restore some semblance of order, only for strife to break out again, almost immediately after they leave the site. The employers ultimate answer rested with the government of the day, to pass laws to restrict and limit the power of the unions, while trade unions had democracy and workers rights, as tools of their trade, backed up by organised obstruction of many kinds. In principal, the managers, retained the right-to-manage but were often obstructed by powerful unions.

The employers equivalent to the unions strike is the lock-out, to close the site down until the problem is resolved. Both sides use the media to publicise their side of a dispute. On the trade union side, there is the potential support of thousands of workers who are prepared to unite behind their leaders and obstruct the actions of the employers until they are forced to negotiate terms. All in all, as good a system as can be found anywhere in the world, though I would say that most of the rewards go to the wealthy side, there is seldom any real depravation for them. The levels of office in the unions, within an establishment, go from shop steward to deputy senior steward and then to senior steward. Shop stewards are workers with work assignments who are relieved from their jobs for the purpose of conducting their duties as representatives. Most union positions are filled by the process of elections, balloted by the ordinary members, as are branch officers and delegates to various committees and other bodies.

Having said that, I spent most of my time exposing dire examples of undemocratic practices by leaders carrying out unrepresentative policies, despite the safeguards provided in the rule book. Some shop stewards used their office as a means of escaping the grinding boredom of repetitive production work. In a labour intensive situation, with thousands of workers, the senior, and deputy senior shop stewards of the manual unions spend all day and every day engaged on representative activities, contacting and communicating with their members. Ironically, sometimes taking advantage of the opportunity to muster support for some form of industrial action - while being paid!

One way of assessing a stewards personal commitment is to note how much time she/he spends on union business, out of working hours, when they are not being paid. Regrettably, most shop stewards hardly ever go to their union fortnightly/monthly branch meeting, despite the fact that such meetings are held at a venue on the factory site or very close to the factory and at a time just after they finish work, so that they do not have to make a return journey from their home, to attend. The importance of attending branch meetings regularly, lies in the fact that policies drawn up there, are applied to working practices in the factory and when this is often done by a minority who dedicate themselves to disruptive action, it produces a tail wagging the dog situation.

This period of time was punctuated by spells of unbridled madness and was unbelievably chaotic. I have heard of workers, when away from the area, who were too embarrassed to admit they were Cowley car workers. It was often observed that the workers were ordinary sensible people as they went about their personal lives but directly they walked through the factory gates, they became idiots who continued to be led into one dispute after another.

There is a clearly laid down Disputes Grievance Procedure, designed to provide every opportunity to resolve disputes before a damaging stoppage of work takes place. The intervals between meetings can either be used to seek a peaceful solution or, as often happens, for each side to intensify the pressure on the other. In the absence of agreement, after the whole drawn-out disputes procedure has been exhausted, each side has the right to take action, the unions to strike with official backing and the employer to impose their will upon the unions. The vast majority of strikes, walkouts, sit-ins, occupations, barricades, in the period covered by this book, were unofficial and not officially sanctioned. It wasn't the status of the unofficial action that was the problem, it was the frequency of its use. I have known eight stoppages, all at the same time, all on different issues.

One reason for this behaviour by groups of workers was because when they returned to work, it was as though nothing had happened. They knew how many days they were on strike and how much money they had lost. They also knew their relationship with the supervisors and managers would be the same as they were before they went on strike. If that was friendly, even polite, that is the way they were when they returned to work. What they did not understand was that contingency arrangements had been drawn up by the company to deal with whatever the management had conceded to end the strike. At this stage the strikers probably felt reasonably satisfied with what they had extracted from the management. They didn't get all they wanted but they got something. The management would not make an announcement about fresh plans, there was no need, and they didn't want to sound vengeful, but the sort of thing they did was, arrange for the strikers' jobs to be contracted out for a lower price, or worse still, when the accumulated cost of settling disputes got to the point, where it was cheaper to close the factory.

A classic case was when some young workers asked for an increase in their pay. They were not apprentices they were called 'improvers', who had just left school without much in the way of qualifications. Sometimes their fathers, having spent a lifetime working for the company, had requested that they be given a job. To cut a long story short, the negotiators on the union side succeeded in getting a £7 per week increase, but the cost of that settlement was such, that the company stopped employing improvers, forthwith and forever. The improvers had priced future applicants out of the market.

CHAPTER NINE
Barricades

---

*Altercations on the factory gates.
The O.R.M.O. appeal for funds.
Barricades interrupt production, we accuse the management.*

Not only did we campaign for the moderates in the internal factory elections, we also campaigned at regional and national elections, and in an undated ORMO-TU leaflet we recommended anti revolutionary candidates and urged workers to vote accordingly

THE AUEW POSTAL BALLOT

ASSISTANT GENERAL SECRETARY	VOTE J.P. WEAKLY.
NATIONAL ORGANISER	VOTE JIM BRADLY

Pass this leaflet to an AUEW Member.
AUEW Members. Keep this leaflet until you have voted.

In the 15th Edition of ORMO-TU dated August 1974, we made a lengthy appeal for funds. It went as follows. *It was the moderates in their thousands that refused to support the old T&GWU leadership, earlier this year when the management took action against Alan Thornett, it was the same moderate, but angry people who demanded the outside officials should come to the rescue and put an end to the costly chaos of previous months.*
So please support this restrained and responsible publication and give your donations to the people whose names appear at the foot of this page or send them to R Gatehouse, Sawpit Road, Blackbird Leys, Oxford.

It was a plaintive appeal that produced five small donations. Taking the final number to four hundred and fifty, and marked the end of financial support by the ordinary union members. The outcome of our appeal did not surprise us, nor did it affect the immediate future of the operation, it was always run on a shoestring, and anyway it was the eagerness with which our leaflets were grabbed from our distributing helpers, that demonstrated their interest in what we were doing.

Union leaders, the members had previously railed against, were deposed by Reg Parsons, aided by new deputy senior stewards, he reduced the strike rate by 92%. This was achieved under the new system, allowing the ordinary union members to vote in the elections for senior stewards, a right denied them hitherto.

Harry Landon, Charlie Hammond, Mont Gibbs and Philip May, all were eager helpers, as they needed to be, to withstand the exposure to the ardent supporters of unbridled militancy, These lads would have been subjected to a certain amount of criticism from some people in the vicinity of where they worked. Actually Philip May did not last long and although he never said at the time, he applied for another job and was transferred to another factory. I always thought it was his way of shedding the stress of being involved with ORMO. While handing out leaflets, there were a few times when one of the opposition would get so mad at me, he could hardly contain himself, and a fierce argument would ensue, which lead me to realise we had found the soft under-belly of these people, and the attack had to be sustained. I must confess to thinking of a couple of well-known sayings, one was 'fortune favours the brave' and another, 'the pen is mightier than the sword'. It now occurs to me, that Thornett could quite easily have had the same thoughts, when he was attacking the employers. We were both fighting for what we stood for.

The most controversial leaflet I ever composed was Edition 23, dated November 1975. It involved commenting on a dispute under the title. 'Discipline. The ADO71 Quality Drive'. Instead of aiming our criticism at the militants, we sided in good measure with them, and 'had a go' at management. *Too severe and unfair, that was the message that came across when the ADO71 (Austin Princess) line workers downed tools and set up a production barricade on Thursday evening (night shift) on the 23 October*. Almost spontaneously these workers put into effect a new weapon to stop management's indiscriminate measures against some workers. Endless pleading by the shop stewards to the superintendent, urging him to reconsider some of the cases, were to no avail. Finally, reality had to be faced by the workers. Tough action was their only logical answer. Whoever started it didn't matter, two stewards stepped in and adopted a positive but responsible policy of sticking to the mass meeting decision, part of which was if a certain worker was sent home on suspension, then the whole of the Princess Line, would stop for the duration of the man's suspension and would barricade key positions until the North side (of the factory) production and rectification would be stopped.

The AUEW shop steward, Herbie Wietz (who was opposed to unofficial organisations that distributed leaflets) and Charlie Hammond, who was a member of ORMO both saw that it was tough enough to be effective but at the same time, were able to prevent the revolutionary agitators from exploiting the situation by extending the strike or increasing the demands. The workers resistance to indiscriminate discipline was clearly demonstrated, and greatly strengthened the hand of the senior stewards who had, until then, been fighting a losing battle of words with the management. The barricade and support it received, forced the management to think harder on the issue. They would be well advised to recognise that no matter what. Even under the threat of job losses there is a point, beyond which, the workers will just not go.

Charlie Hammond tells how a night-shift senior steward who had been called in, and while trying to avert a stoppage of work, (something a Trotsky motivated shop steward would never do) asked the superintendent if he, had made any mistakes, on being told he had, the shop steward asked why, then, wasn't he suspended?

Most workers, some stewards and ORMO acknowledge that some union practices must be resisted by the company's administrators, but it must be done by a recognised progression of measures that will give everyone a time-spell in which they can adjust their behaviour.

The new weapon was how we described the production barricade that was so effective on the North side, (actually, it did not, halt the rectification departments where I worked.) on the 23rd October. 1975. Its use was a sobering experience. It was fortunate that it sobered the management, but it also sobered (almost alarmed) many of the workers who witnessed it, but didn't know what it was about. It so happened I was working nights that week and I notified my supervision that I had clocked out, which gave me the freedom to move about and to keep abreast of events. Technically, I had joined the strike (but not the barricade).

We have sufficient confidence in their final judgement, that most workers will exercise discretion when deciding if and when it is appropriate to use this method of pressurising management Except for a few short lived mistakes, we think workers will know, for example, whether the size of the group contemplating barricading is large enough to be effective. Also whether it will inflict more losses on their fellow workers than the company. The serious consequences, and possibility, of violence erupting must also be taken into consideration, ORMO's coverage of the barricade incident was in sharp contrast to our usual line on industrial action, we have never said strikes should be banned. Most advances in workers welfare have come about as a result of stopping work, if only to get the bosses to the conference table. It's what happens when offers and concessions are made, that divides the socially fair-minded from the politically motivated.

The previous most publicised leaflet was Edition 12, dated April 1994, when we called for the resignation of five senior shop stewards, on that occasion, having caused a massive stir within the factory it was picked up by the local and national press and quoted for days afterwards. This time, when we supported the workers, and spoke out against the management, not a whisper. Added to that, I was challenged by the senior industrial relations manager about the contents of the leaflet. On the spur of the moment, I responded by asking him whether he thought he should write our leaflets.

CHAPTER TEN

Discrimination

> *Was Thornetts intervention thwarted?*
> *An unfortunate mistake.*
> *It all died down.*

A row broke out in September 1981 when a memo instructing the security officers on the gates of the Assembly Plant at Cowley to check the identity of every black person trying to enter the factory.' The memo was allegedly issued by Mr R Coxon, the chief security officer. It immediately caused a dispute that developed into a full-scale complaint by the black workers that racial discrimination was a problem at the factory. Despite the fact that the management had cancelled the instruction, given Mr Coxon a public warning that if it happened again it may bring about his dismissal, plus an apology from Mr Coxon, the workers' representatives continued to press for his removal. They attended meetings in working hours, so disrupting production and threatening the loss of pay to their fellow workers, black and white. It made sense that black workers should get together as a pressure group when there is evidence that neither the management nor the unions have properly safeguarded their interests. Their new organisation - the BL Black Workers' Rights Committee - had identified other examples of shortcomings at their expense. One was the failure to promote black workers to supervisors in anything like fair proportions. Another was the dearth of black workers in the technical field of manufacturing. On the union side the only black worker to reach the modest position of deputy senior steward (one out of seven deputies) held office for the briefest of periods. What I did find disturbing was the way their committee was developing. Their lack of experience in industrial relations and labour organisations meant that they were vulnerable to destructive influences and prone to tactical error. For instance, the demands made as part of a settlement to the dispute, was that Mr Coxon should be removed forthwith, despite the fact that this was his first offence of any kind. When union leaders are called to defend one of their members, in a situation where the member had admitted guilt and apologised, they would never accept dismissal for a first offence, and, very often, not for the second. So the demand that he be dismissed forthwith indicated double standards.

On Sunday 13 September I attended a meeting arranged by the Black Workers Committee at the East Oxford Community Centre. Eighteen black people, one white, plus officers of the Oxford Committee for Community

Relations were present. Alan Thornett arrived later than I and went directly upstairs with one or two of the black leaders, who I recognised as production line workers in QT building, south side. Thornett would probably have been told I was in attendance, because, until he arrived, I was the only white person there. Neither Thornett nor I were there out of idle curiosity. I was there to observe the meeting because it related to a problem at the factory. The reason for Thornett's presence was never made known to me, presumably his discussions had some purpose, but his reason for not attending the meeting once it got under way was intriguing. In fact the person who chaired the meeting was very much out of his depth. It must have been the first time he had addressed a meeting let alone chaired one and I got the impression that the poor chap had been thrown in the deep end, at the last minute. To his credit, he did steer the meeting into accepting the services of the Oxford Committee for Community Relations, to assist the committee in presenting their case to the Commission for Racial Equality. Thornett's non-participation of the meeting followed all previous examples of him ducking out of chairing a public meeting, when I was in attendance.

At a later meeting in the factory, the black workers were persuaded to allow the issue to be placed in recognised grievance procedure, which meant the matter would be dealt with by higher levels of management and union officials.

A letter I wrote to the Oxford Mail, published 23 September 1981 headlined '*Black Workers at British Leyland should have a jobs bias*' and ended as follows, *I would like to see the Leyland management adopt certain measures to meet the present situation. The first would be to operate a temporary bias, when selecting supervisory and technical staff, so that, when all else was equal, to appoint the black applicants and to do this until a fairer proportion of black people hold these positions. Second, I think that the practice of appointing ex-civil police officers to chief officer of plant security should be abandoned. This is not the first time a retired ex-civil police officer has blotted his copybook and left the company. I don't think it works out well at all, the needs and responsibilities of the two jobs are poles apart.*

The above is an updated version of the letter published. To the best of my knowledge, the policy of employing ex-civil police to be chief security officer at the factory was abandoned. Tragically, some time later, Mr Coxon suffered a serious illness that could very well have accounted, and excused his misjudgment at the time of the black workers dispute.

CHAPTER ELEVEN
In Office

> *Examples of Thornetts guile, his strengths, his weaknesses —
> and his deceptions.*

My term of office as a shop steward started in 1968 and ended in 1974, and that was through the most prolonged and disruptive periods of industrial unrest ever seen at the Cowley Assembly car factory, peaking in 1969, when there were 625 recorded strikes.

The unrest had started in earnest a couple of years earlier and went on until the early 1980s, when the annual rate of strikes dropped dramatically. That was due to several factors. Firstly to Reg Parsons' intervention, then the management taking action against the most extreme militants and, finally, the trade union officials who refused to use spurious arguments to support the union members who advocated the slow but relentless dissipation of the company's finances, by strikes.

When talking militancy at the Assembly Plant one is talking 'Alan Thornett'. The time he spent, the volume of printed matter he produced, the travelling, the meetings, the campaigning with others, the arguments with his own union, the interfacing with management. He robbed thousands of workers of wages, lost due to strikes that failed, and was directly responsible for the repeated warnings, given by management, that we were pricing ourselves out of the market in the name of Trotskyism. It was Thornett's genius with exploitation and bluff that carried him on. The exploitation was of weak Boardroom Directors and Management and his betrayal of the ordinary workers' trust in the unions. In my opinion his worst 'crime' was the abuse of democracy. Other trade union leaders left themselves exposed to criticism for going along with him, yet a split took more courage and foresight than any of them possessed, with one belated exception. That exception was ex-deputy senior steward, Reg Parsons, who changed from being a revolutionary Trotskyist leader to being right wing and 'anti' everything he had previously stood for.

A quote by Thornett, on page 13 of his book entitled *Inside Cowley'*, he says, 'a series of strikes and militant actions (including the occupation of the Cowley Assembly Plant by the day-workers) forced agreements to be honoured, despite crippling costs to the employers'.' So there we have it. He knew what was happening when strikes took place, and still he was forever recommending, organising, prolonging, provoking and supporting industrial disruption. One example was when he said, 'I arrived at the department late and found my members, the transport drivers, were already walking out on strike'. We are supposed to think that it was nothing to do with him. Was there no such thing as a telephone call, or a preconceived plan that arranged for it to happen that way? Of course there was.

I will give two more examples of deception. The first describes a situation where a militant shop steward was employed on what was known as the 'control bridge' and this shop steward represented four other workers. The control bridge housed the electronic control panels that activated large areas of the powered automation, such as the moving assembly lines, the conveyers that fed the car body shells to the assembly line, and the overhead conveyers that fed components to where they were needed, for the workers to fit to the cars. To put it in simple terms, the control panel operators 'switched the factory on' at starting time and 'off' at finishing time. This shop steward soon realised that if he wanted something, and the supervisor refused, all he had to say was, my members will switch the controls off, and that happened. That way the dispute was resolved, the shop steward getting what he wanted.

At some stage the senior steward got to know about this facility, and was known to have contacted the control bridge, saying he wanted a stoppage of the assembly lines, (as a means of pressurising the management into submission on some other issue), and the lines were stopped. Needless to say the management had to find a way round this problem, so they offered to give the shop steward and the four control bridge workers, staff status. At first the offer was turned down, which forced the management into negotiations, at the end of which the four workers and the shop steward accepted the new terms offered and changed their membership from the T&GWU to the staff union. This put them beyond the reach of the T&GWU senior steward. Problem solved.

In his book, Thornett blamed the right wing for this 'betrayal by the steward and his four members', leaving readers to assume it was done in Reg Parsons's time, but that is not true. It was done in Bob Fryer's time, under the old militant regime, before Reg became the senior steward. There is a side issue here - it begs the question, was it democratic for one person, even a senior steward, to call upon a tiny minority to interrupt the earnings of hundreds of workers in a dispute that had nothing to do with them? Without consulting them? I think not.

The second example of deception involved the manner in which he was eventually excluded from the T&GWU. I searched his book from cover to cover, not because I didn't know, in fact I did know, but I wanted to see how he had described the event, which after all was as momentous as anything that had gone before, but to no avail. No graphic account of a clever manoeuvre that demonstrated, yet again, his ability to maintain control of events, in fact just the opposite, all he could do was to skulk away with his tail between legs.

Perhaps he under-estimated his readers' interest in the matter. I feel obliged to record a true account of the event in the spirit of comradeship, between two union brothers, Alan and myself.

The situation with regard to the second example was thus. He had been sacked by the company for driving one of their lorries while holding an expired drivers licence, and, horror of horrors, having parked in a no parking zone. He was picked up by the police, and subsequently fined in the local court. The sacking left him in the position of not being allowed in the factory and he lost contact with some of his long-term colleagues. Andy Brown (deceased), who had been an ardent supporter of his, had an arrangement to pay his union subscriptions when they were due and be reimbursed when next they met. The arrangement had worked well for a long time. Then one evening, after Thornett had been sacked, at a very important branch meeting when vital elections were to take place, Thornett made a point of being present. He located Andy and approached him to catch up on his union subs. When asked how much he owed, he was told that he owed nothing and Andy added, 'You are not supposed to be here, you are no longer a member of the union. I haven't had to pay any subs for you'. Thornett left the meeting never to return. In his book he identifies lots of 'defining moments'. How come he let that one go by unrecorded? We are talking here of the ever-winning Brother A Thornett, scourge of the capitalist system, the genius who outwitted everyone from a list of plant directors, local union officials, up to and including, national General Secretaries, not to mention droves of ordinary factory workers.

At the height of the long period of almost continuous strikes and other forms of disruption, the dominant leader of it all said, two or three weeks before an annual holiday, 'we will lay-off now, to give them the chance to earn a bit of money for the holiday.' This policy was not announced in the T&GWU 5/55 Branch News, probably because it was not official union policy. Perhaps it occurred to some of them that it takes rather more than two or three weeks to save for a family holiday. I would have said at least six months. Even that would not have erased the memory of occasions passed, having had to cancel planned holidays because potential earnings, through strikes, were way below what was needed.

CHAPTER TWELVE
Dream World

Thornett looses the plot.
Terminally weakened: The T. & G.W.U. members chuck them out.
The new man steps into the top job and wins an award.

In January 1974, just before the 9th Edition of ORMO-TU was distributed, anyone could have been excused for thinking the editor of 5/55 Branch News of the TGWU, had gone stark raving mad! Had storm troopers entered the factory to round up the trade union leaders? Were we all going to be transported to Siberia? Had a dictator been installed in Westminster overnight? He announced that the branch committee had circulated, in the form of a resolution: *'The only constructive solution to the problems facing us at the Cowley factories, in the event of the employers enforcing sackings or closure, is for the occupation of the plants concerned.'*

Presumably Comrade Thornett, the editor in question, was going to occupy the Plant Director's chair, and then what? Order tea and biscuits for the transport department shop stewards? Change all the factory gate locks, call all of the factory workers in to start the production lines? That wouldn't work. Send out letters to the workers explaining how much better off they were going to be, now that they were in control of the factory? It all smacked of Walter Mitty to me. For instance, the resolution continues: *'Once the plants are occupied we would call for the resignation of the Heath government and the election of a Labour Government as a matter of urgency. The occupation would give us two advantages'*, the resolution says, *'the plant could be held and maintained in good working order, and would give us bargaining power'*. Was that last sentence about maintaining the plant supposed to be a display of reasonable authority?

When the 9th Edition of ORMO-TU did appear, it carried the following response to the resolution. *'Occupation - A Joke or a Serious Possibility - We are against it. We who produce ORMO-TU are convinced that the plan to occupy the plant, if put into operation, would serve to worsen the position. In fact, we regard the thinking behind it to be blindly one sided, based on wildly inaccurate predictions and presented in the form of dramatic rubbish. A Joke? If it was a joke, we question the use of official channels for such an activity but will enter into the spirit of the thing by making the following suggestion. Let us put our grievance into the 'Disputes Procedure' and in the meantime get as much work and pay out of the situation as we can, until procedure is exhausted. The terms of reference should read, that members of the next government be nominated by the 5/55 branch committee of the T&GWU. The time and date of the election to be held on the morning of 1st April.*

ORMO had been in existence for eight months by the time the 8th Edition had been distributed and had become an established entity in the factory as an open challenge to the various revolutionaries. It had also attracted the attention of the Daily Telegraph. On 20 April 1974 it quoted our leaflet under the heading *'Union moderate tries to end Leyland strike'*. The strike by one hundred and fifty car assembly workers had made 12,000 other workers idle. Three quarters of the article detailed a list of measures we proposed to deal with the very damaging strike.

I was pleased with the publicity the organisation was getting, but not surprised. Several lengthy and detailed letters of mine had been published in the local newspapers, exposing the activities of the trade union leaders. Our distribution of leaflets was more thorough and better organised than the other groups and, as I pointed out, we were fellow workers who shared factory life with them, unlike the young college students recruited by the revolutionaries and primed with all sorts of rubbish. Very few of them had any work experience or family responsibilities. Handing out our leaflets on the factory gates throughout the winter days and nights in icy or rainy weather, enabled the workers to see us 'in the flesh' as it were.

For me personally, the whole thing opened doors. I was invited to become a member on the BBC Oxford Radio Council. I joined the Labour party and was made a school governor and anyone I contacted and asked to meet, agreed to do so.

When discussing the arrangements to hand out leaflets on the factory gates we all agreed to take two precautions. The first was, that if anyone tried to snatch the whole bundle of leaflets from us, to let them go and not get involved in any violence. The second was to avoid stepping over the factory boundary line in a manner that could lead to us being accused of distributing on company premises. On one occasion, after I had handed out leaflets at the factory gate, I was called into a manager's office, and, in the presence of an industrial relations officer, was told they had received a report alleging that I had been handing out leaflets on company premises. With a feeling of relief, I replied that I feared it was about text, not territory. I told the manager that I knew the consequences of that possibility and was always extremely careful not to step back inside the gateway while handing leaflets to people entering the factory. I then asked who had reported the matter, expecting it to be a member of management or supervision, only to be told that it was a T&GWU deputy senior shop steward and named him. He was a member of the Workers' Revolutionary Party who, like a little boy, trotted to the management telling tales.

The 13th Edition of the ORMO leaflet, dealt with one hundred and fifty Leyland transport drivers who were on strike in support of their leader -Alan

Thornett. He had his credentials as a deputy senior steward withdrawn by the management. As a relatively small group of people they would have had no difficulty in communicating with the rest of the factory. Yet with all the numerous opportunities, with statements in the newspapers, over the radio and television, in documents by official, and unofficial, bodies, I never saw or heard any statement expressing regret to the thousands of workers and their families for lost wages caused by their selfish strikes. Surely there could have been someone in their midst with the decency to at least express some degree of guilt about the unfairness of it all.

The pleasing news was that the T&GWU enquiry into the whole shameful conduct by two of their senior stewards had resulted in an immediate implementation of a new method of electing senior stewards and deputies. Under a new rule, ballot papers were to be issued to the ordinary members as well as the shop stewards, thus securing a more representative leadership in the future.

As the routine biennial election for the senior and deputy senior shop stewards became due, Bobby Fryer, the incumbent senior steward, and Alan Thornett, an existing deputy, both put their names forward, together with Reg Parsons a new challenger for the office of senior shop steward. The ballot took place with the following result.

Reg Parsons	1,881
Bobby Fryer	824
Alan Thornett	407

Reg had come a long way since he produced a cartoon that appeared in the 5/55 T&GWU Branch News (see page 59). It was about the same time as the Watergate and Richard Nixon scandal in the USA was in the news - hence the Watergate implication. He depicted me, on a pantomime horse, dressed in period costume, sword in hand about to charge the T&GWU Headquarters saying, '*Now we have collected £9, we can thrash them*'. This was his response to the 1st Edition of the ORMO leaflet, when we started a collection to meet expenses. In those days he was a leading figure in the Workers' Revolutionary Party, but he changed to being as outspoken 'against' the revolutionaries as he had been 'for' them. Having won the election, he would hold office of senior steward for two years

In the 14th Edition of ORMO-TU in August 1974, we wrote, '*What a Difference, New Union Leaders, and no Undemocratic Strikes. Reg Parsons, the new T&GWU senior shop steward, had inherited a situation worse than any new leader ever had to face. A membership hard pressed by savage increases in the cost of living but seriously weakened by unpopular and fruitless strikes, plus organised disruption by the people who opposed him in the election The practice of shouting him down at meetings, adds to his difficulties. We need to build union support at the Assembly Plant behind strong democratic leaders who have the sense to keep the membership with them and use its strength in a way that will avoid anti-union rebellions. In the meantime, just to be allowed to work and be paid for a full forty-hours represents a twelve percent increase each week for line workers, on what they were getting in the pre-Parsons era.*

We should remember that Reg was the only man who had the guts to openly oppose the revolutionaries, and stand against them for the senior stewards position, in the T&GWU elections.

We who were responsible for ORMO did not at any time think the industrial relations war was over, we knew that others, all pulling in the same direction as us, had won a battle but not the war.

There is still a long and hard struggle to come. The achievement has been to break the mould of the extremists at the factory, and that is important for the future'.

All sorts of things happened during Reg Parsons' period of office. The local and higher echelons of the T&GWU officials worked with the newly elected factory leaders to maintain the democratic procedures that had been introduced, to protect the members against manipulation. Reg's intervention in the industrial relations at the Assembly Plant had achieved its goal. The old problems were eradicated, even after Reg was defeated two years later, by the old brigade of comrades, who were toothless and racked with desertion and betrayal by the people who took so long to see through their crass stupidity.

I was surprised when no less a person than Bob Fryer approached me as he was passing through the canteen. He asked if I was going to support him in our leaflet for the election for a senior steward, against Reg Parsons, because, he said, Ivor Braggins, another candidate, was still 'in' with the Trotskyists'. I told him that I would not, and he moved on. There was no discussion, and to this day I have no regrets for two reasons. First, because Bob won that election without our help or opposition, and took up the reigns once again as the T&GWU senior steward. Secondly because I would never forgive anyone lightly, who had done so much damage in the past to the source of my, and many other people's, livelihood,

Bob had distanced himself from Thornett, and that was probably because of the event, two years earlier, when Reg Parsons was elected. Thornett stood against him then and split the vote against Reg, We did however, campaign in the election of deputy senior stewards, with the result that three of the candidates out of seven elected were supported by ORMO. Bob Fryer's suitability as a natural candidate to speak for, and represent, British workers, provokes speculation, he was after all, always the senior shop steward throughout the whole period from the late 1950s through to the mid 1970s, whereas Thornett was never more than deputy senior. If various experiences he, and his family, had, earlier in his life, as referred to in one of Thornetts books. Apparently, Bob's early life, started with the fact that his father was a soldier in the Hungarian Red Army. In defeat, he escaped from Poland to Berlin and then ended up in Vienna. In the1930s Austrian fascists took power and established a dictatorship. In 1938 Hitler's army marched into Austria and a year later Bob arrived in Britain, after most of his family had been persecuted by the Nazis and lost in concentration camps. My point is, it would hardly be surprising, if anyone who had experienced such years of torment, through his formative years and on into manhood, that his personality, his character and his judgement, when dealing with capitalists, might have been set, never to be altered. With Bob, we got what we saw, but there had been times, before Thornett out-militanted him, when toilet walls in the factory had 'Sack Trouble, Sack Fryer' daubed on them.

The development of ORMO into an election campaigning instrument was a natural and vital aid to the masses of non-active trade union members, whose main contribution to the unions was the regular subscriptions from their pay packet. They were at work for the prime purpose of earning money to support their dependants and to finance their lifestyle. Their involvement with the unions was confined to contacting their shop steward when they had a grievance or wanted something, while their commitment need go no further than keeping a watchful eye on their elected representative, to check whether he/she is acting in the best interests of their department. As for attending boring branch meetings or giving time to protest marches etc, they thought we who did that were plain daft, or were in it for ourselves.

Edition 18 January 1975. *'We now make a semi serious, tongue-in-cheek, comment on the merits or demerits of the people who as individuals, made the headlines on matters related to the factory, throughout last year.*

Man / Woman of the Year Award? We have decided to award Reg Parsons the 1974 British Leyland Assembly 'Man of the Year' (Industrial Peacemaker Section). We totted up his credits and eliminated his rivals and discovered that no-one deserved it more than him. No full-time union official deserved it because throughout the year they came to the factory, rearranged things and then went away leaving Reg to make it all work and carry the stress, day in and day out. The AUEW union senior steward did not deserve it because of his acquiescence in the activities of the revolutionaries when they dominated us. (I could have added that he tragically failed to protect the good name of his, and my, trade union, by supporting viscous attacks by the T&GWU revolutionaries, on such people as Terry Duffy and Hugh Scanlon, the AUEW national president and ex-president). No member of management deserved it, because if they had conducted their business properly in the past and not waited until a bitterly frustrated work force had torn themselves apart, demanding sound direction, things would not have been so bad. Carol Miller did not deserve the title because her efforts as spokeswoman for the workers' wives amounted to no more than a (admittedly valuable) two-day wonder, and as far as we know, has done nothing since. Carol Miller, together with Margaret Whiffen, were the leaders of a spontaneous protest march to the factory gates by hundreds of wives and families of local car workers, who were constantly being thrown out of work because of strikes and shut-outs.

At the top of Reg's credit was indisputable courage. Anyone who took on the ruthless power struggles within the T&GWU and between the union and management, and work so close to the limits of their ability, as did Reg, deserves recognition.

But then we observed a fault. Reg was trying to carry too much on his own. Instead of allowing a respectable amount of democracy at the branch and in the conference room, he allows himself to be provoked into making dictatorial statements that gets him into even deeper trouble. He should relax a little. The membership, other stewards, the officials and the management now know how to handle the revolutionaries. He must keep his own house in order and cultivate the confidence the membership showed in him when they voted him in.

So that is it. Reginald Parsons - Man of the Year 1974 - will go down in the history of the Cowley Assembly car factory, as the person who was elected to challenge and defeat the most disruptive and destructive shop stewards ever to plague the factory. We in ORMO condemned the previous leadership most of all because of their lack of democracy and, even though Reg's brand of control accords with the membership's wishes and enables them to carry on working, he would find it much easier if he allowed more freedom of expression and confined his control to the implementation of his policies.

Stabilising the industrial relations, and the vast improvement in the average earnings made possible by Reg Parson's willingness to occupy the hottest seat on the trade union side at the factory, adds up to a huge debt of gratitude from workers well beyond the factory boundaries.

Visual Reminders

50 OUT OF TUNE

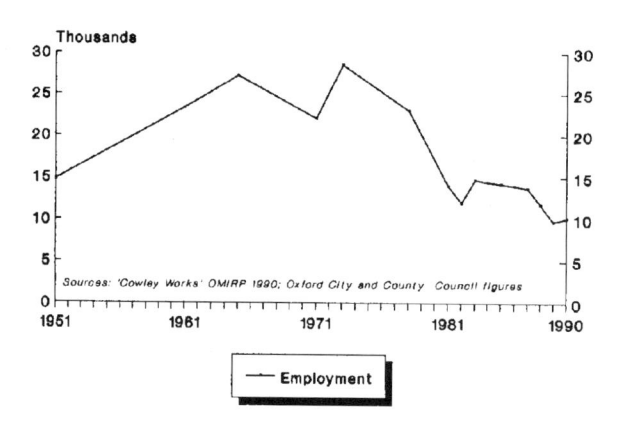

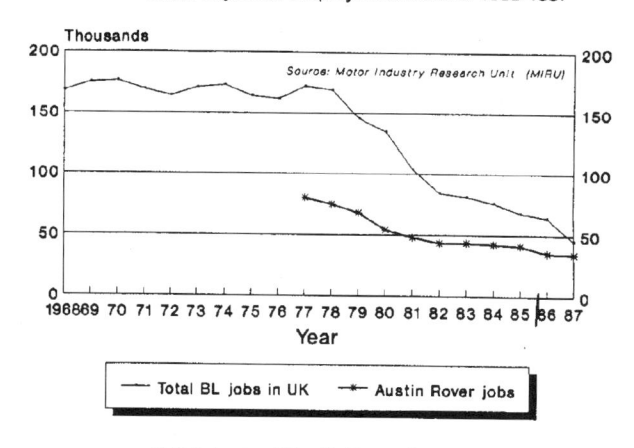

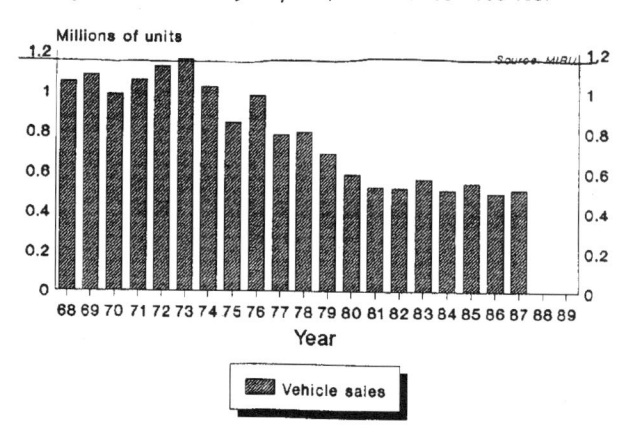

Vehicle Sales and Employment Graphs. Taken from an independent enquiry report chaired by Lord McCarthy of Headington.

VISUAL REMINDERS 51

campaign for Q R year

The year starting October 20, 1966, has been chosen for a national campaign to focus attention on quality and reliability. All the leading organisations in industry have pledged their support. The British Productivity Council in association with the National Council for Quality and Reliability has been asked to initiate and to undertake the general rôle of organisation.

2 Much is, of course, already being done by individual firms ; trade associations, employers' organisations, research associations, representative bodies in single industries ; professional bodies ; the National Council for Quality and Reliability ; the British Productivity Council, with its network of local productivity committees and associations, many of them with specialist sections on quality and reliability.

The Quality and Reliability Year, campaign notice.

> P.T.O. SUBMITTED FRIDAY 12TH DEC 1969 FOR FEBRUARY MEETING
>
> Notice of Motion to be put to the next M.M.J.S.S.C. Meeting.
>
> That at M.M.J.S.S.C. meetings, recommendations from the platform and resolutions that directly concern only Austin and Morris Cars Div., Cowley No^{03} 1 and 2 Factories, should not be spoken to or voted on by members of B.M.C. Service 793.
>
> Submitted by R. Gatehouse
>
> Signed by
>
> E. Martin — AEF   R.G. Werrett — A.E.F
> Cullen — T.G.W.U.   B.B. — N.U.V.B.
> Mawdsley — N.U.V.B.   C.E. Blake — T.G.W.U.
> P.E. Brown — N.U.V.B.   B. — A.E.F.
> Bell — T.G.W.U.   J. Wagg — T.S.S.
> Les Gurl — A.E.F.   F. Hughes
> Sims A.E.F. G.W.U.   L. Wyatt
>   T.S.   J. Hayes

The notice of Motion with the signatures of ten shop stewards that was put before the Morris Motors Joint Shop Stewards Committee.

Brother Les Davies, the 'reliable old timer' whose early days were spent in the Tyneside shipyards, when working conditions were harsh even for those days.

The last two Austin-Morris 1100/1300's to leave the now out-of-date production line.

Twenty-five year service awards ceremony, all received an inscribed watch. Amongst those included are: R Werret, G Elstrop, D Crockford, T O'Sullivan, C Moss, H. Weitz, J Barsons, R. James, C Blake and B Arnold.

```
EARLY MARCH 1972

FIRST BALLOT        SECOND BALLOT

A  HIGGINS     30   A HIGGINS      26
C  BAYLISS     32   C. BAYLISS     39
B  WINSTON     11   R. GATEHOUSE   46
R  GATEHOUSE   48   D. WARD        18
D.C. WARD      14

STEWARDS ELECTED
R. GATEHOUSE        46 VOTES
C. BAYLISS          39 VOTES
```

The Tuning department shop steward's election results. An example of the notices on the departmental union notice boards.

Get together plea to unions

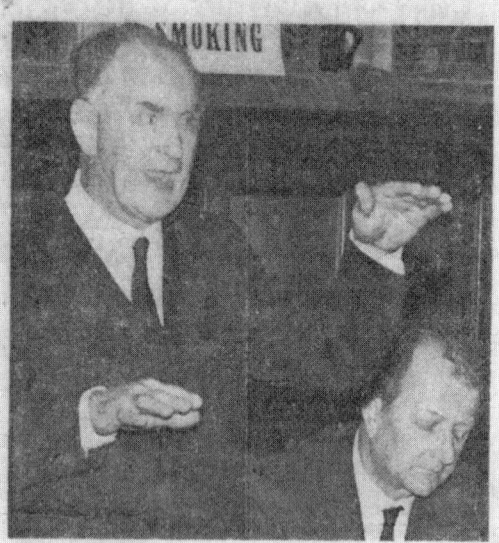

MR HUGH Scanlon, president of the Amalmated Engineering and Foundry Workers Union, said in Oxford last night that there would have to be an end to sections pursuing their own interests in the car industry.

"We have now reached the point where the car industry is so sophisticated and integrated that five men can turn 50,000 out of work," he said.

Shop stewards should be given more authority, works committees should be set up and claims should go outside the factory only when the works committee agreed that they should.

Harming ourselves

He was answering a question from an Austin Morris shop steward, Mr Roy Gatehouse, who said: "We have now got the situation that I can't see us getting in a full week's work and the people who are doing us most harm are our fellow workers.

"The only answer is some form of co-ordination which means restriction. This problem now is on everybody's lips. We have to have some sort of policy on getting together and not destroying ourselves," he said.

Earlier Mr Scanlon, talking on amalgamation, asked: "Do we need 22 unions to build a motor car?"

He said he wished there were stronger pressures to bring the vehicle builders' union closer to the AEF.

'Ridiculous disputes'

"It is well known that the motor car industry is controlled by three unions. Whoever gets the vehicle builders virtually controls for trade union purposes the motor car industry."

Mr Scanlon attacked the "ridiculous demarcation disputes that go on between us."

"What working-class outlook is there in a demarcation dispute? All that we do is weaken ourselves by these ridiculous disputes.

Mr Hugh Scanlon, president of the AEF, speaking at the Oxford Union last night.

Brother Hugh, later Lord Scanlon. He addressed fellow members of the Amalgamated Engineering and Foundry Workers Union in Oxford. The author was in attendance.

TO : THE ASSEMBLY PLANT EMPLOYEES

Fellow Workers,

For some time now I have been thinking that there is a need for an organisation at the Assembly Plant that represents moderate opinion on trade union affairs and it is with this in mind that I have taken the trouble to distribute these letters.

In an establishment like ours, where the unions have so much influence in our working lives, standard of living and future employment, it seems wrong not to have such an organisation.

There are several left wing socialist groups which operate very effectively representing the views and interests of those who believe in Marxist/Trotskyist policies with the resulting imbalance of influences being brought to bear on the Plant leadership. I believe the lack of support for, and loyalty to, the Trade Union leaders that is evident sometimes at the Assembly Plant is partly due to the degree of militancy that they display on some factory issues and more particularly on political matters.

No-one can dispute, since the Government has introduced the law and wage restrictions into our working conditions, that politics are in trade union affairs to stay. To some degree they always have been, but many ordinary workers would rather settle the political issues through the ballot box, at the local and national elections for political leaders.

An organisation to represent moderate opinion could provide a voice for all the people on the factory floor who wish to support the trade unions without the fear that their support will be interpreted as being evidence of a desire to strike on every failure-to-agree or case of political dissatisfaction. It would provide an opportunity for the mass membership to support the trade union movement in return for the many agreements that have been won for them and for the pay levels that must be at least £10 per week higher than the employers would be paying if it had not been for the union organised pressure.

The plant-wide movement that I envisage will need support in several forms. One could be merely to contact me with your views on the value of such an organisation, secondly to assist with the administration and thirdly, sufficient financial aid in the form of small donations that would be paid straight into an account, open to view, to ensure that all monies are properly accounted for.

If you see no immediate need to support my idea, keep it in mind that casual support would be welcome and can be built on.

Roy Gatehouse
(North Side Tuning)

17 Sawpit Road,
Blackbird Leys,
Oxford.

The Open Letter to the factory employees, announcing the launch of the Organisation to Represent Moderate Opinion, in Trade Unions. (O.R.M.O.-T.U.).

Dear Brother Gatehouse

Supplementary to my official letter enclosed, as you are aware, in my personal capacity, I am a member of the "Engineering Voice" Oxford Committee which I prefer to term a progressive organisation working towards socialism with the idea of encouraging mass participation of workers towards achieving that aim

I thought it best to add this note because I did not feel I could insert same in an official letter, yet at the same time I did not wish to give any false impression about my personal membership of this unofficial Committee

Yours fraternally
Malcolm Young.

Unofficial letter from Malcolm Young, District Secretary, referring to my intention to set up an unofficial organisation (O.R.M.O.-T.U.).

The cartoon attempts to redicule the results of our first appeal for funds, by the time O.R.M.O.-T.U. was disbanded, we received 450 donations, which included three five pound notes.

The author (circled), attending a 'Kill the Bill' demonstration in London, against Barbara Castle's (Labour) 'In Place of Strife' legislation.

A demonstration through Oxford against the Norman Tebbit's (Conservative) industrial relations Bill in the early 1980's.

DONT VOTE FOR CAPITALISM 5-1-78

Almost two million unemployed, industries destroyed, hospitals closed down, education undermined and unprecedented cuts in living standards. How is it that the working-class of this country, constituting the majority, has allowed itself to be subjected to these attacks?

We must all have wondered whether or not anything will change after the next election. Labour? Tory? Liberal? They are all as bad as as each other. What happens to all the election promises showered upon us? What do the politicians at Westminster have in common with the interests of the working-class? What incentive are we given by any government to do a self-respecting day's work? To vote for any party is to vote for the continuing destruction of Britain. The Labour government is as bad astthe others: by destroying our Health Service, our industry and our schools it attacks the working class whom it claims to represent. For how much longer will we go on voting and giving this mandate to our class-enemy?

If we, the working-class, were in control would we run our country like this? Of course not. We must therefore seize control and rid ourselves of the parasites who are destroying British industry and the working-class — the capitalists. The only answer is to replace capitalism with a socialist Britain, governed by the working-class for the working-class.

LABOUR = TORY = LIBERAL = CAPITALIST.

DON'T VOTE , ORGANISE FOR REVOLUTION.

To discuss these issues further please come to a public meeting organised by the C.P.B.M-L. at 7.30 p.m. on Tuesday October 10th at the Cowley Community Centre.

READ THE WORKER.
p &p. Communist Party of Britain Marxist-Leninist.
155. Fortess Road. Tufnell Park. London N.W.5.

Typical of thousands of communist leaflets, distributed for many years, aimed at persuading workers to support the communist party.

3rd Jan 1973 ACTUAL DOCUMENT, POSTED

After two meetings between the Tuning Shop Stewards (at the first the Seniors were present) it has been discovered that the T.&.G.W.U. and the A.U.E.W. at Senior Steward level, cannot agree to a common approach on how to present our claim to 'Go-Skilled.'

The T&G refuse to support the A.U.E.W. on the 'Skilled' issue and have instructed their members in accordance with that policy.

The A.U.E.W. Stewards are seeking a further meeting with the A.U.E.W. Senior Steward to work out a plan on which to proceed.

Further information will be made available as the matter developes.

The notice displayed on the Tuning Department notice boards, on the first claim for skilled status, which was abandoned on the grounds that the Transport & General Workers Union opposed the claim.

These ladies did just what was needed, they were instantly supported by hundreds of other factory workers wives with their families, and were able to put their case to John Symands, the factory director.

A pub setting for an *Oxford Journal* photograph, from left, Brothers, R. Atherton, D. Devlin, unknown, and E. Mortimer, 30th January, 1976.

The A.E.U.W. Union district office, now closed and restored as two separate shops. The bay windows over numbers 171 and 173 Cowley Road, formed one long committee room.

Mr. H. Weitz,
Secretary,
Cowley 203 CE Branch.

Dear Sir and Brother,

Ballot Voting for District Committeeman July/June 1975/76
Cowley 203 CE and Oxford No.2 Grouped Branches
―――

Please find appended below details of the Ballot Voting in the above election -

Name of Candidate	Branch Voting Returns	
	Cowley 203 C.E.	Oxford No.2
Gatehouse. R.	46	13
Soanes. M.J.	35	8

As the Return Sheet received from Cowley 203 CE Branch shows one more Ballot Vote cast than the number of signatures on the Recording Sheet I, as Returning Officer, have had to declare invalid the Votes cast in Cowley 203 CE Branch.

Brother R. Gatehouse is therefore declared elected as District Committeeman by 13 Votes to 8 Votes, with Brother M. J. Soanes as Provisional Representative.

Yours fraternally,

M. W. Young
District Secretary

The District Committee Election Results – the first time.

John Arnold, popular and respected, as a person and as a shop steward.

68 OUT OF TUNE

A Trotsky success — or a Board Room failure?

The author with Bill Morris, General Secretary of the Transport & General Workers Union.

Bernard Moss at work in the senior stewards spacious, but temporary union office, in the B.M.W. Cowley car factory.

Bernard Moss (left), the Transport & General Workers Union, senior shop steward at B.M.W. Cowley, together with John Barrett (centre), former chairman of the old Assembly Joint shop stewards committee and Ivor Braggins, Regional Officer of the T. & G.W.U.

The author in the new B.M.W. Mini.

Shop stewards and members of the T. & G.W.U. 5/837 Branch. Back row left: J. Glen, M. Taylor, A. Paintin, N. Harris, unknown. Front row: R. Parsons, K. Blake, C. Blake and J. Barsons. Neville Harris became a full-time union officer, for the T. & G.W.U.

It was Reg Parsons who defeated Bob Fryer in the election for senior shop steward, and by doing so, broke the mould and culture of destructive militancy that had contributed to the downfall of the British car industry at Cowley. His transformation from rabid revolutionary to something completely opposite, terminally weakened the militants.

The author with his wife Barbara, taken while she was serving as Lord Mayor of Oxford.

CHAPTER THIRTEEN
Thornett Breaks the Rules

> *A copy of a statement in Alan Thornett's book* 'Inside Cowley' *page 275. A strike by his own transport department drivers.*

BL (British Leyland) lorry drivers were not involved in the strike, as such. We were a part of the BL Wages Structure, not General Haulage. We were known in the industry as Own Account Drivers but once the strike started we refused to touch any goods normally moved by those on strike. Cowley was quickly closed down by the strike due to a shortage of components from Llanelli, South Wales, normally transported by general haulage (GHA) drivers now on strike.

Management demanded that we fetch the components but we refused to do so without the agreement of the South Wales Strike Committee and the Plant remained closed. Then Management obtained a letter from the T&GWU Regional Secretary in South Wales, George Wright (who had been the right-wing candidate in the General Secretary election). In his capacity of Secretary of the Central Strike Committee of Wales, authorising our lorries to carry goods from Wales normally carried by general haulage vehicles now on strike. Wright argued that this was in order to put pressure on Road Haulage employers. The policy of the Central Committee Region 4 South Wales is that all Own Account vehicles are allowed to carry all work normally carried by RHA firms not in dispute. This is to bring further pressure on the RHA firms to settle at £65 for 40 hours. Therefore based on the above policy British Leyland drivers and lorries can move between Wales and Cowley all loads including anything normally carried by the RHA firms still in dispute on the clear understanding that RHA firms that settle at £65 for 40 hours be returned to their normal work. After checking the letter's authenticity, a fleet of lorries left Cowley for Llanelli to collect the components and re-open the plant. We told the drivers before they left Cowley for Llanelli, that if challenged by the pickets on the gates of the Llanelli plant they should not go through but phone back. Percy Trinder, the steward for the long distance drivers, was going, so it hardly needed mentioning. Crossing a picket line had never occurred to him. Late that night he phoned to say that there were pickets on the gates at Llanelli who were saying that Wright's letter had nothing to do with them. I phoned the night manager in Cowley to tell him that the night drivers were not going through. He was furious and said the drivers had two choices: They could go through the picket and pick up the components or they were off the clock (would not be paid, and uninsured to drive the vehicles RG) and could make their own way home. The drivers refused to go through the pickets or return to Cowley and next morning, after a battle, management relented and allowed them to drive back empty.

It can be seen in the first line of the quote above, that the BL drivers were not involved in the Road Haulage strike. In fact, from the time George Wright, the T&GWU Regional Secretary in South Wales produced and forwarded a letter to BL Management, who had passed it to Thornett, it was obvious there were no grounds for BL Drivers to refuse to pass through the picket at Llanelli. Wright was carrying out official policy of the Central Strike Committee for Wales, and Llanelli is in South Wales. In the meantime, while all of this was going on, the Cowley car factory was at a standstill because they had run out of the components that came from Llanelli.

The workers at Cowley were not asked if they were prepared to sacrifice wages to support the Road Haulage Association drivers, or told that the T&GWU at national level had authorised the British Leyland drivers to pass through the Llanelli picket lines. I have acted as a picket with others on picket lines and I have crossed a few of the unofficial variety. There would have been no disciplinary action against the drivers for crossing the picket in those circumstances. So what was the problem?

Thornett overreached himself on this occasion, which was no accident. He was running true to form, he was doing what he always did, fighting the management, working-off his warped ambition to dominate anyone who operated the capitalist system.

What bothers me most about all aspects of this dispute was the way management dealt with Thornett. They should have stuck to their guns and ordered the drivers to stay there pending further instructions. More than that, they should have forbidden them to drive their vehicles back to Oxford unless it was loaded with components. The drivers, having their personal, social and family life disrupted would have had them scurrying back to Oxford on the company terms, as quickly as they possibly could. They did not mind disrupting thousands of other workers' lives but they would not make any personal sacrifices themselves. An opportunity for the management to step in between the transport shop stewards and the drivers, by imposing their terms, seemingly never entered their heads.

What the management did was capitulate and in so doing incurred the cost of running a fleet of empty lorries to and from Llanelli and, in the process, pay the drivers (plus their overnight accommodation) while the production workers were shut out, without pay. On top of that, they actually delayed the whole process of restarting production, because they still had to wait for the components to be delivered by some other means.

Why weren't the Cowley union members asked if they were prepared to sacrifice wages to support the Road Haulage Association drivers, after having been told that the T&GWU at national level had authorised the British Leyland drivers to pass through the Llanelli picket lines? At times like that, workers must wonder if there was ever, anyone on their side.

CHAPTER FOURTEEN
Downing Street Comments

My defeat in the tuner's shop stewards elections.
The Tuning Department Dispute.
The Prime Minister, The Right Honourable Harold Wilson comments.
A definitive disaster.

In April 1969 I was elected AEU shop steward and held office for five consecutive years representing the Tuning department. Records show I was unopposed on the second annual election, opposed on the third and fourth years and, in the election for the fifth year, only just scraped back in. As the sixth annual election approached, I knew I was in danger of being defeated. I had become somewhat flippant when approached by the members, due I think to an overwhelming feeling of fatigue. I'd had a busy five years - as a steward in the department, attending the fortnightly branch meetings, (none of the other Tuning stewards bothered, except for the odd special occasion), and all those things that I have already listed. I was proactive throughout the Quality and Reliability Year Campaign. Every year I had organised the fundraising for, and distribution of, the Old Peoples' Christmas food parcels. I was on the Trades Union Council, Oxford Radio Council, as the editor of ORMO. Each year I campaigned in the run up to the annual municipal elections (which took a month and made me late with our garden) and, on top of all that, I would grab as much overtime as possible at work.

Being a mechanic, we always owned secondhand cars, which meant doing my own repairs, and I remember one year, having prepared our 1946, Series E, Morris 8 for its M.O.T., taking it to the service station on the morning we were due to set off to Devon for our annual holiday. Fortunately it passed the test.

It was fatigue that plagued me on the run up to the sixth annual election to stand as a Tuning shop steward for another year. As the date drew close, I began to realise that I would miss the satisfaction of holding office and set about producing a manifesto. It was a programme full of plans and good ideas. I produced enough copies for every AEU member in the department and distributed it at lunchtime, trying to drum up support as I handed them round. When the result of the election was known (I lost by two votes) I thought perhaps they had remembered the flippancy. I enquired and was told 'You spent too much time away from the department' another way of saying that I had neglected their interests. Unfortunately, my long-standing friend, Charlie Bayliss, was voted out at the same time, probably condemned for his association with me. It was obvious the Tuners wanted some action and thought they were loosing out because of my preoccupation with the factory-wide fight against excessive militancy. Basically they were wrong but it had to be proved to get it out of their minds.

The Oxford Mail, on 23 May 1974, published the following account of my electoral defeat with the heading '*Protest steward defeated. Mr Roy Gatehouse, the man who first voiced shop floor disquiet at the Cowley car assembly plant when he publicly called on the senior shop stewards and their deputies in the T&GWU and AUEW, to stand down and seek re-election, has been defeated in an election for a shop steward. He was one of the two representatives for the AUEW, in the Tuning department in the North works who were replaced by two newcomers in a shop floor ballot. Apart from saying that he was very surprised at the result, Mr Gatehouse declined to comment. Mr. Gatehouse and Mr. Lawson Bayliss, the other tuning steward, have been replaced by Mr Roy Jefferies and Mr Ken Parker.*

Invariably when I experienced a setback, I would console myself, first by thinking that if they (the represented) did not trust my judgement, that was a pity and I was disappointed. Secondly it gave me an opportunity to spend more time doing things with my family. I still had the ORMO-TU leaflet, I still attended the union branch meetings, there was still the letters to the Oxford Mail and last but not least, I still had my job at the factory.

At about this time, I was approached by one of the communist members of the district committee who was also a member of my branch to see if I could do anything that would stop the Tuners from seeking support from the District Committee, which was the next step towards making the strike official. I took a dim view of the underhand way that was sought to deal with the dispute. The District Committee should have been seen to refuse to support the strike if they doubted the chances of a successful outcome. I did not say as much but just replied that it was beyond my control. I was no longer their shop steward. I had saved them from themselves once before, in 1972, and was still thought to be in the wrong. The new Tuning stewards had got themselves embroiled in what was destined to become, a hopeless mess. They met powerful resistance from the union side before they had even met the management, and they, seeing the disarray, refused to concede anything, let alone the demand for upgrading. The disputes procedure was followed through, with long spells between meetings, each at a higher level of management and trade union officers, until the procedure was exhausted without agreement, after which, the AUEW members, decided to strike, which it did.

On the occasion, of the month-long strike, I found myself a job as a mechanic in a back-street garage and while there, I responded to an announcement through the local media calling for the Tuners who were on strike, to attend a meeting in the Cowley Workers Social Club giving a day and time. When the time of the meeting arrived, I was at work, in my filthy overalls (this garage was the type of place that repaired old cars where the underneath was covered in black oily grime) and set off as I was. The only concession I made to tidiness was to remove the worst of the grime by washing my hands. To go to this meeting in that mode was deliberate and calculated to show my 200 pro-strike colleagues that, because my resistance to the strike was ignored and defeated, it demonstrated my ability to shield myself from the ravages of wanton unofficial strikes.

The meeting was addressed by a national officer of the Engineering Union, a left-winger by the name of Reg Birch. Also on the platform was Malcolm Young, the Oxford District Secretary. Two hundred and five members were in attendance.

In his opening address, Brother Birch made the point that once a national officer has been called in, the control of the dispute is in his hands. After he had finished his address the meeting was thrown open for debate. I raised my hand and was invited to speak, at which point Malcolm Young left the platform and went in the direction of the toilets, sometimes the timing of such an incident can be seen as a gesture of disrespect to the person speaking, especially as the meeting had only been open for ten minutes. That sort of thing was of little consequence. I spoke for twenty minutes in favour of calling off the strike and closed my speech, but not until after Brother Young had returned to the platform.

I can't remember who else spoke, it had been a bit of a strain, but I do remember the result of the vote, which was conducted by a show of hands, ninety five supported my proposition to end the strike and one hundred and five voted to continue the strike. There were five abstentions. With all the publicity strikes were getting, I thought it likely that journalists would be hanging around the front entrance, so I opted to leave the venue by the back of the building.

The Tuners dispute was a classic example of how negligent the main participants were in dealing with the problem. Those involved were Doug Hobbs, deceased, the senior shop steward of the AUEW, the District Secretary of the AUEW, and four of the five Tuning shop stewards, the two officers for failing to warn the Tuning members of the hopeless nature of the claim. It was never justified because one third of the department were employed doing things like adjusting the windscreen washer jets, bleeding the brakes, adjusting the odd finisher and anything that could be rectified on a short length of the moving conveyor. It was weak not to point out that, with all the adverse publicity and general hostility from their fellow workers, and the determination by the management to crush the Tuners, they should have introduced a damage limitation strategy. Instead they chose to preserve their reputations for macho militancy.

The Oxford Journal, 30 January 1976, published a lengthy article headlined '*Jubilant Tuners Prepare to Celebrate their New Status*,' accompanied by a photograph of four of the Tuning leaders celebrating with a pint, in what looks like a pub (see page 65). I can only think that the pints they were holding must have been at least their tenth in succession, and that a very rosy glow accounted for both their jubilation and their account of what they had achieved. To admit finally that 'no (extra) money was involved' makes me wonder whether the tuning members would have been so eager to strike if they had known that in the first place. The settlement as announced was that the Tuners had been allowed skilled 'production worker' status with no extra payment, a grade that was not recognised by the AUEW rules, and a meaningless status that was never implemented. As the original resolution that 'All Tuning members to be upgraded from semi skilled to skilled' be submitted, that was the only item covered in the claim. The biggest shock was still to come, it even bemused Doug Hobbs, It came in the form of a statement from the management saying that they intended to reduce the tuning department to one third of its original strength', leaving two thirds to be moved out and no longer part of the department, the smaller group to remain in the tuning bays where the big, more interesting jobs like changing engines, suspensions, wiring harnesses and other major strip down and rebuild work, would be done. Tuning was never the same again. In the past if the management had been so foolish as to tell the senior stewards that, without any consultation, they intended to cut the manpower in a department of two hundred workers by two thirds, all hell would have been let loose, an instant call for strike action by the whole workforce, urgent phone calls to General Office at 110 Peckham Road, the lot. Instead there was bewilderment, resignation and a feeling of helplessness.

While all the machinations were going on, when the Tuning stewards were awaiting developments, other, unskilled workers of both unions, moved in and were helping the management to clear the rejects that were normally the preserve of the Tuners. There were T&GWU and AUEW, members openly and gladly working away, including my branch secretary, no doubt many of them remembered the days and weeks when they were shut out without pay, while selfish Tuners were striking for something they never had any chance of achieving.

The Oxford Journal, a local newspaper, 24 October 1975, headlined on its front page: *'Tuners ready for fresh showdown' The Cowley tuning department is ready for another crippling showdown with British Leyland. Their shop stewards say the 250 Tuners are fed up, frustrated and totally despondent. They feel that the arbitration which persuaded them to call off their strike eight months before, was a complete con trick'.* 'The Journal', continued, *'They made themselves the most hated group of workers in Britain when they went on strike to support their claim that they should be reclassified as skilled men. They were attacked by the Prime Minister The Right Honourable Harold Wilson, by almost the entire British Press and by politicians of all parties. They suffered abuse from their own neighbours - and some even from their own families.*

The Oxford Mail, on Monday 30 June 1975, wrote; *'In the seven years since Leyland was formed more than eight million man hours have been lost through internal disputes at Cowley - 6.4 million in the assembly plant - 147,000 hours were lost because of the Tuners strike'.*

As for Roy Jefferies, the person who took over as shop steward by defeating me in the election, he took redundancy and by doing so, created a vacancy in the show-bay that I filled the day after he left the company, and occupied for ten years, until I took early retirement in 1991, having completed thirty two years, not counting twenty two months on the production line between 1954 and 1956.

CHAPTER FIFTEEN
All Change

> *Barbara and I move house.* • *I change to another union branch.*
> *Barbara opens her Ice rink.*
> *For the second time, I am elected onto the Oxford District Committee.*
> *Strange voting statistics.*
> *The closure of the Engineering Union's Oxford District Office.*

Barbara and I moved from Blackbird Leys, the council estate that was close to the Cowley Car factories, to Headington. This was a suburb of Oxford that had expanded, encompassing the two small villages of Old Headington and Quarry Village, each retaining most of their old stone cottages, numerous stone walls and alleyways. Many of the buildings that are now trendy dwellings were once barns, farmhouses and stables. All are made to blend with newly developed housing and amenities. The move eventually prompted me to transfer from the Cowley branch of the union, to the Headington branch which had a history of being anti communist. That changed after the branch secretary died. His position was taken by Alan Jeffcote, a skilled man who was the convenor (senior shop steward) representing six hundred and fifty toolmakers in the Body Plant.

Barbara, an Oxford City Councillor, happened to be chairperson of the Recreation and Amenities Committee, and, in that capacity, lead the move for the Council to take over the project started by Oxist (Oxford Ice Skating Trust) the local Ice Skating Club, to build an ice rink. The club had raised thousands of pounds towards the cost, but were forced to face the fact that their target was unachievable and so appealed to the Council for assistance. The appeal was passed to Barbara's Committee and, with her enthusiastic support and persuasion, the committee voted to make funds available that would cover the difference between the Ice Skating Club's balance, and the overall cost. Within thirty-nine weeks of starting the construction, the Ice rink was up and commissioned.

I was totally supportive of Barbara in her council activities and in this regard I joined Oxist and was obliged to obtain a membership card with a passport-type photograph. Both were obtainable at a council office in the city centre.

In 1984, the situation at the factory had altered a great deal. The rate of strikes had massively declined due to the clearout of many of the revolutionaries, plus the submission and conversion to moderation by some of the others, with the predictable result that the management were retrieving more of their old territory by demanding more stringent conduct from the workers. One diktat came down from on high, to the foremen and managers, stating that no workers were allowed to leave their workstations without their authorisation. One likely reason for the measure was to reduce the contact between shop stewards and the workers, which had been so effective in the past, when union activists were setting the agenda. (I was charged and received a recorded warning for leaving my department without permission, when caught campaigning on behalf of moderate candidates at election time). On another occasion I was ordered out of a department by the supervision because militants threatened to call a stoppage of work, if I was not made to leave immediately. So we all did the same sort of thing, and it was all good knock-about stuff!

Once again, I thought it would be useful to be the delegate for my new branch, on the district committee and I got the chairman of the branch to nominate me as a candidate to stand against Alan Jeffcote, the branch secretary. There were about four hundred members in my 'new' Headington branch. On the evening of the election, there were five people in attendance when the branch opened for business. Those present were Bill the chairman, Alan Jeffcote (secretary), Terry Hall, John Arnold, and myself. John was a friend of mine, and I asked him to attend the meeting to vote. He came and voted for me, the chairman voted for me and I voted for myself. The secretary (Alan) voted for himself and Terry voted for him. So Alan scored two votes while I scored three. It was something of a coup, because Alan's position as secretary of the branch with four hundred members and as convenor representing six hundred and fifty skilled men where he worked, should have assured him of plenty of support. I wasn't even a shop steward. It was too early for celebrations because there was another branch to ballot.

The system for electing branch delegates to the district committee was the same as it was at my old branch, namely that one delegate represented two branches and so both branches held ballots for the one delegate. It meant that Alan Jeffcote and I faced another election by the other branch. It so happened the other branch was a night shift branch, which meant that their branch meetings were held in the daytime - 10 00 a.m. in fact - while I was at work, and so, bearing in mind the management's diktat, I wrote to Malcolm Young, the district secretary and told him that I would not be able to attend the daytime branch meeting, to observe the ballot because of the company ban on taking time off on union business. I asked him to tender my apologies and to inform the other branch secretary, that I would not be able to attend the meeting on the day of the ballot. He did not reply but I presumed the message had been passed on.

About a week or so went by and the day of the second branch ballot arrived and I was at work as usual. At about 9.30 a.m., I approached my department manager, Dave Ward by name, and asked for permission to leave work as I had some council business to attend to in the city centre, saying I would be back at

1.00 p.m. I relied on his knowledge of my wife's high profile on the Oxford City Council and that I frequently accompanied her to functions, plus the fact that I had a good working relationship with him and so he acquiesced to my request. The 'Council business' that required my presence was to acquire an Oxist ice rink pass. The route to the centre of Oxford, from the factory passed along the Cowley Road and by the AUEW District Office, where the ballot was taking place. I was making the journey on my bicycle and when I reached that point at about 10.00 a.m. the voting was due to start.

The union premises consisted of two old fashioned, small-fronted shops (see page 65), one with a small back room which was used as an inner office while the shop functioned as a reception area. The rest of the premises, which was the larger part, were taken up with a staircase leading to a long conference room across the top of the two shops. There was also an anti room at the back, plus the caretaker's quarters. The rear of the premises was accessed through a side entrance, separate to the shop door. This enabled callers and the caretaker to enter the premises unseen by anyone in the union office, and without their knowledge. Having parked and secured my bike, I entered the union premises via the side entrance and went upstairs to the ante room where the ballot was to take place. As I entered the room I noticed there was only two people present, the branch chairman and the branch secretary. I introduced myself by name and took a seat that was tucked away in a corner that was as far out of sight as possible from the entrance to the room.

The chairman explained that the ballot had not started because of the absence of the people needed to make the meeting quorate. After a while one person arrived to vote and was told that there was a problem and that if he cared to call back in an hour or so, it might be possible for him to cast his vote, Time went on. No other branch officers arrived to make the meeting quorate and I felt obliged to point out to the chairman that the ballot was invalid if it remained the way it was. This fact was acknowledged. As the time was approaching twelve noon the member who called earlier to vote was turned away as before. It was about then we heard the sound of someone approaching via the stairs, preceded by the voice of Brother Malcolm Young. While still not in sight of me he asked, *'How is it going, chairman?'* (I never did know that chairman's name) *'This ballot is invalid because the meeting is inquorate'* replied the chairman. By then, Malcolm had stepped far enough through the door to see me, and I, too, made the same point. *'Ah ha'*, says Malcolm, *'just a minute, rule such and such says the branch can stay open for five hours'*. *'Just a minute, Malcolm'*, says the chairman, *'I'm not staying, I've got a dentist appointment at.12 o'clock.'*

Malcolm's last chance, to either phone around or to visit two or three people to get them to attend and make the meeting quorate, and to overturn my one vote lead, was lost. Before I left the district office I composed a note, which read *'The ballot that was to have taken place for the election of a delegate to Oxford District committee was abandoned because the meeting was never quorate'*. I got the branch secretary to sign it. As I left the union premises, I showed it to Malcolm Young. I stepped out of his office, collected my bike, cycled into the Oxford city centre, was given my ice skating club pass, cycled back to Cowley and clocked in at 1.00 p.m. at the end of my lunch break. Then was the time for celebrations.

A few days later, I was duly informed by post that I was the elected delegate for two branches, onto the Oxford District Committee.

It proved to be a remarkably coincidental event, because it led to me being in attendance on the District Committee when Malcolm Young informed the committee that he had been offered early retirement. With the reduction of the labour force in the Leyland Combine - indeed the whole engineering industry - the AUEW as an organisation, had to massively scale down its costs and liquidate some of its assets. The membership numbers and subscriptions plummeted and union office sites closed. It was with this background that Malcolm, at the committee meeting, announced that Head Office had told him the Oxford District Office was to be closed and one of the options was for him to take early retirement; the administration of Oxford would be transferred to Banbury. The subject was discussed in detail, with each committee member agreeing the conditions that suited Malcolm, including the level of the financial settlement. I felt that the mood of the committee, after the initial shock of the office closure announcement, was such that we were all pleased for Malcolm's sake that he was shedding the burden of office, and had achieved what he wanted. However at the next committee meeting, when reporting on the subject of his retirement, he said he had been contacted by Head Office and told something to do with the arrangements that was not to his liking and caused him to withdraw his agreement to retire early. The response from Head Office was that they would accept his withdrawal from the agreement to retire, but it would mean that the alternative was for him to accept a post in the divisional office at Luton, Bedfordshire. Malcolm retired and the Oxford District Office was vacated and closed.

CHAPTER SIXTEEN

Victimisation

> O.R.M.U.-T.U. disbands.
> John Arnold victimised by the factory union leaders.
> I produce and distribute an 'Open Letter'.
> Friends at Head Office of the A.U.E.W. at 110 Peckham Road, London,
> John wins!

Soon after the publication of the 27th Edition of ORMO-TU, dated June 1976, the organisation ceased to exist. Harry Landon retired after three years and two months, having been the most constant helper/organiser and friend of the ORMO team. Harry, an intelligent, well-organised bloke, did his full share of leafleting on the factory gates without fault or fuss and was a campaigner in his own right. He wrote pungent letters to the editor of the Oxford Mail, adding to the chorus of people who were fighting to drive the destructive elements in the unions, out of office.

The other helper/organiser was Charlie Hammond. He chose to drift away as the need for help faded. We were glad of Charlie's help when active support was demanding and rare. He never lacked belief in what ORMO stood for, but once, when he was collecting donations for the organisation and listing the donors names, he left the list unattended on his bench, only to have one of the opposition pick it up and hand it to the people we were campaigning against. This was a serious breach of confidentiality because ordinary people were worried about intimidation. A similar situation occurred when Brian Jackson, a T&GWU member, joined ORMO at our inaugural meeting. When composing the first publication of the new unofficial organisation, I listed Brian's name, together with that of two others and my own. Consequently, he was threatened with disciplinary action by a T&GWU deputy senior shop steward, and that was the last we saw of Brian.

ORMO-TU as an organisation had served its purpose well. We had produced 79,000 documents:

500	Exploratory open letters
4,500	Three Early editions @ 1,500.
48,000	Twenty-four remaining editions @ 2,000
10,000	Five Un-numbered Election Specials @ 2,000.
8,000	Four Birmingham-produced ORMO Leaflets. @ 2,000
8,000	Four Birmingham-produced Open letters @ 2,000

plus considerable media coverage. ORMO-TU publications were a constant annoyance to the people it exposed.

The annoyance was best illustrated after a particularly disgraceful event that was orchestrated by a small group of shop stewards at a Joint Shop Stewards committee meeting. I exposed the matter in Open Letter No 4, dated August 1985, and was handing out the open letters to the workers as they arrived to start the day shift when a well-known T&GWU shop steward and I had a full-blooded exchange of views on the subject I had exposed. I was told afterwards, that on one occasion when a contentious issue had been raised at the Joint Shop Stewards committee, the chairman cautioned the proposer saying '*Gatehouse will only 'make something of it'* in his leaflets'.

I was comfortable when ORMO-TU had to be disbanded, I still had a means of communicating with the readers of the Oxford Mail through the Letters page and with the factory workers because I continued to produce ORMO-TU under my own name. Collections were discontinued, and so I was obliged to accept the assistance of a rightwing (moderate) group of AUEW members in the Birmingham area. They agreed to produce the leaflets at 2000 a time and deliver them to me for distribution. I wrote the text and they provided every thing else. It meant that I had to do all of the handing out on the gates - 2000 letters at seven factory gates on both day and night shifts.

ORMO-TU publications ceased altogether after the October 1980 issue, having competed with the T&GWU 5/55 Branch News, the Marxist 'Organiser' the British Communist Party and numerous other militant publications, on one side, and the management's letters to the homes of the workers on the other. We were all struggling to influence the ordinary workers after years of open warfare on the industrial relations front. All but a fraction of the British motor industry had been handed over to foreign manufacturers. In short, we maimed our own industry until what we had left is thriving only because it is under Japanese, German, French or American direction. The 'Open Letter' that took its place was addressed to 'Brothers and Sisters', Cowley Assembly, (Austin Rover Group).

There was one more channel of communication that I had developed, and that was by telephone direct to 110 Peckham Road, London, AUEW Headquarters. I had got to know one or two of the union officers there and was able to bypass the district office. This access proved useful in the climax of an attempt by the senior shop stewards and others to have the credentials removed from a shop steward who had done no more than upset them by associating with me. The shop steward's name was John Arnold (see page 67). He, too, was in charge of a store, as was Harry Landon, (of the ORMO team,). John's store served a different section. We were both shop stewards, lived on the same council estate, (Blackbird Leys), were both members of the Labour Party and were both party activists. John and I operated together in all of the official Labour Party activities for twenty years. He was popular and respected for everything he did. As a shop steward he got it exactly right. His members were unflinching in their support for him when he faced the annual shop stewards elections. John did not show any interest in ORMO-TU and I tentatively sounded him out on the subject on one occasion. I think he disapproved, which disappointed me, but there was no criticism of it or opposition to it.

When I described John as being a steward who got it exactly right, I was referring to his brand of militancy. He knew how to extract the most out of his supervision. I remember him telling me how he dealt with a case where one of his members was called to the foreman's office about his lateness and absenteeism. Management wanted to sack him. John described the member as someone who was not bothered what happened and had to be talked into putting up some sort of defence in the presence of management. Before it had got to this stage, his supervisor would have gone through the process of seeing if there were any domestic or personal reasons for the man's difficulties. Once it had been found that there were no other problems the union was called in. John got the bloke off with a promise to mend his ways. The member broke the promise and was once again in front of the management who still wanted to sack him. John did his stuff again and got the bloke off again. This went to the third time. By then, John felt he'd had the rug pulled from under him and had to give up. The bloke was sacked. Some would say John had wasted his time, but in many cases of that kind, the charged person would have taken advantage of the second or third opportunity and was able keep his job, and forever after thanked John for his help. John had a built-in sympathy with his fellow workers and always sided with them. Another reason for his popularity with his members was because he would scotch any proposed strike action advocated by the political outcasts. His mates (members) always sought his guidance.

The following item is an updated leaflet I distributed on the factory gates, two thousand of them, for the purpose of shaming the leaders of both main unions

Open Letter No. 4. ARG Cowley Assembly.

Brothers and sisters: I had hoped to avoid criticising the T&GWU shop stewards in this issue, as there are other matters of an urgent nature involving the AUEW that I am anxious to tackle, but recent events dashed these hopes.

Before the summer holiday, after much delay and many urgent requests from both the AUEW and the T&GWU senior stewards, the management agreed they should be allowed to call a joint shop stewards' meeting, in working hours, to discuss the company's proposal to bring into effect a new disciplinary procedure.

When the time for the meeting arrived and the shop stewards had assembled ready to start, the T&GWU stewards collectively objected to the presence of two AUEW stewards who had worked during a (unofficial) strike. They said the joint meeting of the two unions should be abandoned if the two stewards, namely John Arnold and A.N.Other, insisted on their right to attend.

All of the AUEW stewards withdrew from the meeting place to discuss the situation. It was then that more pressure was put on the two stewards, first by a deputy senior steward and secondly by a leading group of their own stewards, who said they would boycott any AUEW meeting attended by the offending stewards.

John Arnold and the other steward, as a matter of principal, and quite rightly, said they would continue to attend all meetings where their steward's credentials provided entitlement. When the situation was reported to the T&GWU stewards, they implemented their decision not to meet with the AUEW and in fact stayed on and discussed the management proposals on their own and the AUEW stewards left the meeting place. Now certain facts need pointing out:

Fact No 1. The management have since imposed the new disciplinary procedure with the shop stewards having wasted an opportunity to jointly argue for changes and safeguards at the proposal stage. Once again the Assembly Plant stewards have provoked a settlement by imposition rather by discussion and amendment.

Fact No 2. Both of the AUEW shop stewards were officially recognised by their union.

Fact No 3. Both stewards have been re-elected since the November strike.

Now some questions.

Why didn't Ivor Braggins, the T&GWU senior shop steward, who advised against victimising the two shop stewards, exercise his authority by overruling the bully boys, by so doing, respect the right of another union's members to pick who shall represent them at meetings? Does this now mean that the AUEW can exclude T&GWU stewards with whom they disagree?

Why didn't Doug Hobbs, the AUEW senior steward, do his job and defend the principle and his own two stewards who were under attack. Worse still, why did he stand by and watch his deputy try to pressurise the two stewards to abandon their commitment to represent the people who elected them?

Perhaps the most important question: was John Arnold targeted, for his association with me? It stands up well to reasoning. The whole business of causing a split between the two unions, at a time when the senior stewards of both unions had, as is recorded in the first paragraph of this 'Open Letter', after much delay and urgent requests, frittered away an opportunity to protect jointly the membership's interests in a situation where the company had indicated a tightening of disciplinary procedures. (Why would the militants insist on instant action against two shop stewards who could have been dealt with systematically afterwards?) End of quote.

It did not end there. The AUEW senior steward processed the complaint against the two stewards through the District Committee right up to National Committee.

This is where I arrived on the scene. I telephoned 110 Peckham Road, Head Office to tell them that, among other things, the strike involved was unofficial and that both stewards had been re-elected by their members after the incident, with a very sound majority.

The AUEW District Office was notified that the case against John Arnold was rejected. Those who were trying to get John's shop stewards credentials withdrawn were thwarted in their attempt. I believe a prominent T&GWU senior steward was behind the whole episode. My intervention in this matter gave me the opportunity to reward John for attending the branch meeting and casting his winning vote when I was elected for the second term as branch delegate on AUEW District Committee.

CHAPTER SEVENTEEN

A Triumph from Honda

> *The Honda experience.*

When Rover announced that they had entered into an agreement with Honda to produce what was to be called the Triumph Acclaim it was the beginning of a totally new and beneficial experience for the Cowley car workers. One of the early measures taken to adapt the car to European needs was to create more legroom for the rear seat passengers. It is accepted that the Japanese people are less tall than European; so that design feature had to be adjusted. The reaction by the workers to the differences between Leyland designed cars and the Honda designed Acclaim, was mixed. It ranged from criticism of the thinness of the steel in the body panels to approval of the superb neatness when the panels were attached to the car. The 'gauge' (thinness) referred to by the workers was judged by the old concept that thinness equated with weakness and *vice versa*. In fact, the strength of steel is determined by its quality. Leyland introduced the new, high quality, thinner steel with the Maestro and Montego models.

An insight of things to come was evident when I was talking to a foreman, who was booking in the supply of Honda components to build 10,000 Triumph Acclaims. What astounded him, and me, was the lack of extra items that Honda had provided to allow for losses, mishaps, etc. When he queried the matter and mentioned spark plugs as an example, he was told there was one spare spark plug to cover the whole contract. It was in sharp contrast to anything we were used to. When we started a new model, there were spare components, including expensive items lying around all over the place, especially in the rectification areas. That is the way the Japanese worked; their efficiency and attention to detail nullified the need for extra spares on a large scale. Cowleys performance (I am referring now to many years ago), resulted in a high percentage of the cars coming from the production lines having to be routed to rectification departments.

After the Acclaim came the announcement by the management that there was to be a further joint venture with Honda. It involved the design of two large cars, one to be called the Rover 800 and the other the Honda Legend. The two cars were the same except for certain body design features, interior upholstery and the instrument panel. The production plan was that Honda would build its Legend and our Rover 800 in Tokyo for sales in the South Pacific Region, and we would build Rovers for the European and North

American markets and Legends for home and Europe only. A date was set for both companies to launch the models simultaneously. As time went on, it became clear that Rover would not be ready by the agreed date. Rover had to tell Tokyo that they needed another six months. Presumably, Honda went ahead with its launch.

Eventually, production at Cowley got under way. The launch went ahead, and it was then that problems started. Cars sent to America were developing faults. The very hot Californian sun was bleaching the colour out of the front crash pad; and the front screen rubber seals were shrinking and letting in water. The American agent, who had been involved in the arrangements and had been talking of 50,000 cars, was out of touch. Cars were accumulating at the various ports due to the failure by someone, to arrange for their distribution. Other makes of cars there were stored undercover, while ours were outside and suffering from exposure to the elements. This situation continued long enough for another problem to arise. Cars that stand in one position beyond a certain length of time develop flats on the tyres that are permanent and cause vibration when the car is in motion. All of the cars with this condition had to have the wheels changed.

Teams of people were sent out to rectify the problems. In the end, some of the cars were passed to leasing companies and then taken back by the company and sold as second hand. To terminate a venture with that amount of investment, and potential, amounted to another massive failure. It was a disaster.

The contract with Honda was to build 10,000 Legends and they were being built on the same assembly line as the Rover 800, at a lower rate: For instance, in 1988 when the Rover production reached the 50,000 mark, only 1290 Legends had been produced. Some time later when I checked, the chassis numbers of the two models, the Rover was in the region of 150,000 and the Honda Legend was at 4000. The Honda was not very different to the Rover but everyone seemed to favour the Rover. The inclination to 'buy British', against all the odds, was still quite strong within a minority of the motoring public.

Honda insisted that, when the Legend cars left the assembly line, they were routed to another moving conveyor that ran over an inspection pit and staffed by Honda inspectors and rectifiers. It was Honda's way of ensuring its high standards of quality. One area of Honda dissatisfaction was the thickness of the paint, the external colour coat and lacquer. The optimum thickness for quality and durability is 300 microns according to the Japanese, and they insisted it be adhered to. Leyland had a serious problem with this, and prevailed upon Honda to raise the figure to allow a slightly thicker layer of paint. The Honda inspection management were adamant for a start, but, for once, they relented and conceded another 50 microns, which is about the thickness of a cigarette paper. Rover were not observing the Honda standard on the 800s because of complications when a fault appeared in the paint inspection area or paint damage occurred. In either case, the car, or the painted body shell, had to be rubbed down and put back through the paint spray booth to receive another coat of paint, which put it over the optimum thickness, especially if the car or body shell had to go through the repair system two or three times.

There was a constant battle between Leyland management and Honda. Leyland management, often with some justification, would protest to Honda about an unreasonable demand. One day our supervision checked a Legend that had been down the Honda inspection and rectification line and picked out a car that had been passed off and ready for dispatch. They removed the 'passed' sticker and sent it back round to go down the line again and, when it got to the end the second time, the history card showed it had been rejected and rectified, after having passed the first time. This example of inconsistency was presented to Honda by Leyland management, but it made no difference. Solid as a rock, Honda took no notice, and no action was taken. Leyland was not always wrong, and Honda was not always right.

After the contract with Honda for 10,000 Legends had been fulfilled another contract was entered into, to build a further 5000 which was reduced to 4000 and then terminated, and that was the end of that.

It is easy to criticise the management of the day, and appropriate to counterbalance the criticism by examining the background and history of their position. Even with an admittedly scant knowledge of the details, it seems patently obvious that when the leaders of the two main companies - The Nuffield Organisation and Austin - came together as The British Motor Holdings in 1952, they did so in an atmosphere of mutual hostility and destructiveness. In Graham Turners book *The Leyland Papers* he quotes Leonard Lord (later Lord Lambury) as saying he was determined to 'screw Nuffield into the ground' and as saying to a senior Nuffield executive that he intended to 'take Cowley apart, brick by bloody brick'.

In my time, Morris's experimental department, the 'jewel in the crown' of any successful car factory, was transferred from Cowley to the Midlands. It was at Cowley that the Morris Minor, the Mini Minor and 1100/ 1300 models were designed, developed and first produced. The Morris Minor is still being refurbished and rebuilt today in considerable numbers as loveable and useful little runabouts. It competed against the Austin A30, which has long since been forgotten due to its mediocrity. The Mini needs no description beyond saying that it was a world beater and deservedly was a candidate for the international Car of the Millennium' award, while the 1100/1300 range won the Car of the Year award four years out of seven.

Austin lumbered Cowley with the Farina (Italian designed) family car that had a steering system that was twenty years out of date, a body style and performance that was uninspiring to say the least. That model had no less than five different company badges: Morris, Austin, Wolsely, MG and Riley. In Lord Nuffield's day, each of them would have had their own shape and styling, not to mention status and reputation. I concede that Austin's conversion from side valve to overhead valve engines was ahead of Nuffield and resulted in several Nuffield models changing to the more efficient Austin engine after the merger.

Before the Second World War, Rover cars were described as 'the working man's Rolls Royce'. Rover designed and developed the world famous Land Rover as an answer to the American 'Jeep'. Austin produced the Austin Champ, which was anything but Champion and fell by the wayside.

Fortuitously for the good name of Morris, the next two mediocrities carried the Austin badge: one was an Austin Westminster, a large car with a self-levelling suspension system which was designed to keep the car level from left to right and fore and aft. The idea was to prevent the car leaning out when going round corners at speed. A hydraulic pump was activated to equalise the level of the car at all times. A problem arose when going rounds two bends in quick succession, an S bend, for instance, in which case the levelling system was still adjusting to the first bend when the car was passing through the second and was actually tipping the car over. Instantly complaints were made. One irate customer parked his car outside the Cowley gates when the factory was closed and refused to drive it any farther. The other mediocrity was the Austin Princess with a four-litre Rolls Royce engine. That did not live up to the Rolls Royce connection.

Squabbling, destructive top executives, with malice and spite, dismantled a proven experimental department and, from then on, in my opinion, failed to match the Nuffield reputation for forward and innovative design and development.

The level of investment in the British motor industry was dwarfed by what was happening in Europe at that time, and even more so by what was happening in Japan. In the early 1960s, we had a Borg Warner liaison officer by the name of Rudi (Borg Warner manufactured and supplied us with automatic gearboxes) who was subsequently transferred to a car factory in Japan. He was there for a number of years and when he returned for holidays and refresher courses he visited our department and would tell us what it was like in Japan. He spoke of the enormous scale of the development that was taking place. He said it was unbelievable and frightening. I remember reading that Fiat were demolishing one of their car factories and were updating it for the third time since the end of the war. The disparity seemed to epitomise the attitude of the British towards industrial investment, particularly in the field of engineering.

Whilst coping with costly strikes and the obstructive activities of the factory union leaders, hundreds of millions of pounds, some of it public money, had been invested in such things as a new paint shop in the neighbouring body plant and the overhead conveyer to the assembly plant, but the approach was piecemeal with expensive facilities attached to 1920s buildings. It was always as a reaction, no more than an attempt to stop the retreat from a manipulated and bolshy workforce instead of attacking the problem (not the workers I hasten to say) and being in control from the start. How come Nissan, Honda and Toyota can come to this country and produce cars that sell like hot cakes without all the problems we have? It is because the Japanese at the very top know how to run their industries and their employees: they run them for Japan. They do not let minorities in the unions run (or should I say, run-down) their industries.

CHAPTER EIGHTEEN
A Downward Spiral

Wrong doings in the Quality Control Department.
I have a skirmish with a top director.
Shoddy after sales service at the local agents.

The mass production of modern motorcars to a sustainable high quality standard in design, finish, reliability, durability, performance on the road, comfort of the occupants, and security, at an affordable cost is a challenge in the extreme.

For the workers, the task of reaching the quality standard by their personal effort, and to carry out that requirement hour after hour, day in and day out, week in and week out, for thirty-nine hours per week, is demanding. It is necessary, both commercially and to provide reliable employment for many thousands of workers all over the country. For some workers, £16,000 per annum is better than any other option open to unskilled people in the Oxford area, up to the age of 45 to 50 years.

The achievement of good quality by the workers can only come about with their co-operation, and that co-operation can only be achieved in a context where all other requirements are in place. Many times over the years, the poor quality of the Cowley product contributed to the year-on-year shrinkage of the company's share of the new car market.

Those of us who worked at the factory for decades saw plenty of practices that contributed to the lowering of quality standards. An incident that springs to mind was when an inspector on the assembly line observed a sub standard fitment on a car and refused to 'pass it off'. When told by a line supervisor to pass the item as satisfactory he refused and explained that the person he was answerable too, had issued clear instructions and he was doing as he was told. In the end, the inspector was removed and replaced by another who was prepared to pass the fitment as satisfactory.

Actually, that first inspector was caught up in the perpetual squabble between the numbers men and the quality men. The former had better promotion prospects for achieving high volume figures, while the latter would get on better if he kept his head down, and let it go.

When a senior manager authorised the refusal of a batch of five hundred vehicles to be passed off as fit for dispatch, he was hauled before someone who the unions referred to as an imported hatchet man, and was asked why the vehicles were not being sent to dispatch. The manager in question, who was responsible for quality control, replied that they failed the quality checks and that he would not allow them to be dispatched until they had been rectified and 'passed off' by his staff. The impasse resulted in the quality control manager being escorted to the factory gates, and he had to contact a higher authority, before he was restored to his original post with his responsibility for the quality of the product still intact.

It was interesting to note that everyone who knew these particular quality managers respected them for their principled stand against the bullish 'numbers' people. There was another case where a production manager moved a quality control manager from his job over exactly the same sort of disagreement. The quality control manager again was cleared of any fault and returned to his post, and the production manager, who was eventually promoted to Plant Director, admitted privately, to being wrong on that issue.

I once had a skirmish with a director. It happened when the company embarked upon a massive communications exercise involving the whole workforce, by laying on a film show and a talk and a questions session. This involved turning one of the factory buildings into a theatre by blacking out the windows and providing sufficient chairs to seat five hundred people. I always tried to take advantage of an opportunity to speak to the top people in those situations and always tried to find something that I wanted an answer to. On this occasion I had heard of something that I strongly disapproved of, and, when the time came, I was given the microphone. With great trepidation I asked them why they (the company) were promoting people from foreman to manager on the strength of the foreman having removed reject labels from production car windscreens (which meant that the car had been rejected and was not ready for dispatch) and then routing them to the dispatch department? At this, the director exploded, the audience groaned and then he started. 'That doesn't happen', he said, 'I would sack anyone that did that'. I was a bit shocked and very nervous, but I had no inclination to withdraw my statement. However, I did not have the nerve to expand on my knowledge of the matter and the director continued to pace to and fro across the stage still denying that it happened, scowling at me in a ferocious manner.

Removing reject labels did happen quite often, and I wondered if my exposure of the practice embarrassed him. These meetings were probably monitored to assess their effectiveness as a communication exercise, and that would account for his anger. It was very significant that at the next briefing session six months later, Doug Dickson, the Plant Director, addressed the meeting and when it came to question time said repeatedly that he would take questions on anything anyone wanted to ask. But I kept my head down and studiously avoided another 'fools rush in where angels fear to tread' performance. A footnote to the above is that the person who was the subject of the promotion soon afterwards was absent from work with nervous exhaustion, probably due to being promoted to a position beyond his ability.

The most frequent response at the questions session involved complaints raised by the employees who had bought one of our cars and was getting sub standard after-sales service from the local Leyland dealers. Each time details of the complaints were listed and an undertaking given to investigate the problem. This was repeated a couple of times. It was noticeable that no progress was being made; and in the end, an announcement was made that no more questions on after-sales service would be taken. End of story.

The question that should have been asked was why was nothing being done? Why didn't the agents put right what was wrong when the Leyland hierarchy had repeatedly raised the matter with them? Did they ever suggest, if Leyland were to put their house in order and stop sending out a sub standard product, that there would be no problem? Then, when the Plant Director was dealing with the employees' complaints, he could quietly ask the meeting who built the cars in the first place?

What is the point if our car design team, striving to compete with the rest of the world, when, having done so, the factory where the cars are produced, for a host of reasons, are unable to make a good job of turning the design into competitive reality?

The classic example was the Rover coded the SD1. The design of the car in 1976 was well ahead of its time. It was priced originally at under £9,000 and won a European Car of the Year award and must have been ten years ahead of any other mass-produced car in that category at that time. It had a beautiful, chunky, rounded back with large rear lamp clusters, a sloped tailgate and a massive rear window, which completed the stylish appearance from behind. The front sloped forward and down to the narrow slit headlamps, side and flasher lamps, giving it a superbly sleek profile that was copied by others and continued to be so for years thereafter. It had a 3.5 litre V8 engine or a choice of three more versions, a 2.6 litre straight six, a 2.3 litre straight six and eventually, a two-litre straight four O Series

Having designed and got a winner into production, what happened? It had water leaks, paint and rust problems and a reputation for being unreliable. Finally, it was taken from the Rover Solihull, which was a new factory built on a green field site, and transferred to Cowley, but by then it was too late. We had given our competitors too much ammunition to use on customers who ought to have been buying Rovers. The buying public does not forget or forgive being sold poor quality vehicles, especially when there is better on the market. It amounted to one more wasted opportunity. Subsequently, the SD1 factory was closed, I believe as the result of failed labour relations leading to poor quality workmanship and too many strikes.

Towards the end of its long production run, it was engaged in a head-to-head challenge by BMW the German car producer, for being the fastest top speed, mass-produced car in its class. At that time, the top speed of the SD1 3.5 Vitesse was around 130 mph; BMW would achieve 134 mph in its car; Rover would go out and do 136 mph in the SD1; BMW upped its performance slightly once more. This was taking place at the time of the Frankfurt Motor Show. Finally, Rover squeezed 139 mph out of the SD1 and then, under wraps, slipped the car onto the Rover stand at the Frankfurt Motor Show and were then able to claim the title of 'the fastest car in its class' on BMW's own doorstep. This tale illustrates how the car was an all-round winner, with a sales potential to match, wasted by the appalling performance of the Solihull factory.

It was demoralising seeing motoring correspondents being less than kind about our vehicles. Seeing our share of the new car market declining, year in and year out, seeing fellow workers at the factory, friends and members of the family being hard-headed and buying foreign cars in preference to ours. Above all, constantly working under the threat of being put out of business because not enough people did their job to a reasonable standard.

The claim that faulty components from suppliers were responsible for failures could be overstated, as a glib attempt to pass the buck. Component faults may reflect an undermanned goods inward inspection department, yet another false economy on the part of management.

CHAPTER NINETEEN

Mistakes Repeated

> *Two enlightening statements.* • *Rotas for everything.*
> *Who leads — the shop stewards or the management?*
> *Taken apart, brick by bloody brick.*
> *They ask, 'How much longer can it go on?'*

'The Cowley car plants, particularly the Morris Assembly Plant, have rarely been out of the national political focus for the last 30 years. In the 1960s and 1970s, the Assembly Plant alone averaged over 300 strikes a year, with a record 625 strikes in 1969.'
Alan Thornett, deputy senior shop steward, in the Introduction of his book *Inside Cowley*.

'In the seven years since British Leyland was formed, more than 8 million man hours have been lost through internal disputes at Cowley, 6.4 million in the Assembly Plant and 1.8 in the Body Plant. The unions say the early losses were a lot less.'
John Symonds, Plant Director, Leyland Assembly. *Oxford Mail,* 30 June 1975.

The two statements corroborate each other. The consequences of the strikes mentioned in both statements should have been readily predictable: they were confirmed by time. Nobody seemed to be learning lessons. Thornett mentioned 30 years. How long ago was it that we lost the ship building industry to the European and the Far East shipyards; the Heavy Goods transport industry (lorry and juggernaughts) to Scandinavia, Germany and France? How long ago was it we lost the motorcycle industry? I was a motorcyclist in those days and the bikes we made were always plagued with oil leaks, among other faults. This doesn't seem to be a serious problem, but it is when the riders have their shoes and trouser legs smothered in engine oil every time they made a journey. We couldn't even compete in the moped industry. The German NSU Quickly flooded that market, as the Honda 50 did later on.

Car manufacturing was surely the last straw. Honda, Nissan, and Toyota have invaded our industry and set new standards in the process. My experience in the Cowley factory led me to recognise, before I retired, that the Japanese have shown us how to run an industry, how to create and build quality motors in double quick time, in every sector of the business.

It was not only strikes that cost the company so much, it was all of the other activities that were so debilitating for the creative and technical staff as well as the supervision, not to mention the product distributors, agents and sales people. Such things as the demand for a rota to be drawn up that allocate tasks to the workers in such a way that preferred and the disliked jobs were shared by all. I have a document that I produced and displayed on the trade union notice board in my department on 25 April 1973, when I was a shop steward, and it lists these rotas. They were as follows.

1 Shut out with full pay. (Shut out means sent home or told not to come to work)
2 Shut out with 80% pay
3 Night shift Rota
4 Weekend Overtime Rota
5 Evening Overtime Rota
6 18 gate Rota
7 18 gate night shift Rota
8 Engine change Rota
9 G K Building, Absentees and Lateness Rota
10 G K Building, Night shift Weekly Replacements Rota
11 Employees Bay Rota

Supervisors (foremen) operated the rotas. They had the task of contacting every worker whose name was next on the list, instructing people to do the disliked jobs and offering jobs on the favoured list. It meant they spent hours contacting people, all on a non-productive activity. This practice operated mainly in the rectification areas.

Rota one was a very costly agreement: full wages, but no production. Rota two was the same as one, except 80% wages were paid for stay-at-home workers. The other nine categories were examples of the inflexible nature of workers who were pandered to in the name of fairness nannying in the extreme. There was also the practice of people brewing tea and having snacks, at all times. There were the 'allowed' collections of money by shop stewards in working hours, for colleagues who were absent from work due to long spells of illness, or for people who were retiring, getting married, or collections for striking workers at other establishments. We had a collection for someone who 'lost' his pay packet (twice) until we discovered that it was not the 'mislaid' type of loss but a gambling type of loss. They were a good-hearted lot, but it was all out of place!

I wonder how many people would like to be able to turn the clock back to the days when they were on factory wages, hours and holidays. I also wonder if they would have behaved differently if they knew how drastic the jobs' losses would be. It took a change of attitude by the factory senior shop stewards, the intervention by the T&GWU full time union officials, like David Buckle and Ivor Braggins (the latter had changed his occupation from being a shop steward inside the factory by being appointed a full time regional union officer). Also Oxford City Councillors, and Bill Morris, the T&G General

Secretary. Finally, The Right Honourable Andrew Smith, Oxford East's Labour Member of Parliament, who acted on behalf of the whole of the Oxford area. They all played their part, in the process of salvaging the Pressed Steel Body Plant, but none of the Assembly Factory survived.

This book, among other things, is about leadership. It was fate that landed the Cowley car factories with Alan Thornett, plus the misguided or weak fellow union leaders around him. The misguided were other militants who refused to curb the excesses of Thornett. The weak made no effort to stand up to him and acquiesced to everything he did, safe in the knowledge that they would survive by agreeing with whomever they were talking to.

I see managers, executives and directors as potential leaders. The higher they are in the pecking order, the greater their responsibility to the workforce as well as to the company. The fortunes of the workers depend on leaders. Leaders succeed by their ability to influence, be it the union leaders or company administrators. At Cowley, the unions had more influence with the workers than the company.

We had only to look at two trends in the existence of BMH as applied to the UK operations. One was the share of the new car market, which eventually started to tumble and continued until we reached the present position, and the other was the failure to match the European car manufacturers' investment programmes. A third trend was the perpetual reduction in the number of workers, from 198,000 to less than a quarter of that figure.

The past failure of British industries should have taught someone on the trade union side a lesson or two. The lack of confidence by the financing institutions in the British workers' attitude to work and industry was always behind the lack of adequate investment. The workers (as a separate entity from the unions) were scapegoats. They were blamed, unjustifiably because they were not in control. It was the factory union leaders that were in control. The workers were manipulated to the point of abuse, and punished by the people who, quite logically, refused or restricted further investment.

The Board of Directors was the destructive party. Their stewardship, from the days when BMH was formed, denied managers the authority to 'manage' the workforce. They knowingly watched the management being dragged along by militancy in the trade unions. The directors' response was to accept the starvation of investment as a form of punishment of those workers. Their inefficiency dissipated the assets of the corporation, while they were on generous salaries, with untold perks.

What Michael Edwards did, British Leyland should have done earlier. His responsibility extended beyond the shareholders, beyond the workers, to the municipalities and the nation as a whole.

Anything of that magnitude, if under attack, should be protected with the same vigour as it would take to contain any hostile force. These 'top people' as I call them, see us workers as bolshy, uncontrollable and self-destructive. That is precisely how masses of people behave when frustrated because they don't like the (union) leaders that dominate them and, at the same time, see the directors neglect the very task the are commissioned to perform.

We, the workers, were bursting to be rescued from the revolutionaries at that time. For years thinking people used to wonder how much longer the company finances would stand the losses. The toughest thing about influence and control is having the confidence to impose necessarily strict rules, not punishment, but rules. If a practice is inefficient or destructive, then insist that it be eliminated. If the union leaders obstruct the measures needed, then shut up shop until the employees make up their minds whether it is better to work somewhere else or to accept the rules. If the management have got it right, the employees will recognise the fact and settle down. If the management have got it wrong, then change the managers. The union leaders are subject to re-election, and that position sometimes precludes giving the best advice to his/her followers. Then is the time for the management to move in, to fill the vacuum.

CHAPTER TWENTY

Reflections

> *A miscellany of Items.*

On page 18 of his book *Inside Cowley,* Thornett described ORMO-TU as a *wacky outfit, a useful back up to the mainstream right-wing operation inside the T&GWU*, and described me as a smug right-wing AUEW shop steward. On another occasion he described me as a dinosaur in social attitudes, because I criticised the Organiser, an International Marxist Group leaflet, by saying *'they had finally sunk to the level of using four letter words and supporting the advancement of homosexual behaviour.'*

The very first comment he made to me, after the publication of my first letter to the editor of the *Oxford Mail,* questioning the wisdom of the union's excessive use of strikes was, *'I would lock you up if I had my way'* and called me a bastard, which happens to be a flagrant contradiction of the information on my birth certificate.

Hollow pronouncement
When ultra left wing union officers say *'companies should invest more in the workers'* especially after they have done nothing to protect those same workers from ill-conceived strikes that has caused massive losses in wages and jobs.

How things have changed
In response to my letter, in the Oxford Mail, inviting people to tell me of their experiences at the factory, one person told me that when the run down of the Series E Morris was taking place, and the introduction of the new Morris Minor was starting, the workers on the Series E were receiving piecework rates of pay, while the workers on the new Morris Minor were on basic rate, which was much less. The story goes, when the pay packets were handed out some of the Series E workers, shared some of their higher wages with the Minor workers. A quaint and generous act of comaraderie, that somehow does not fit in these days.

Cynicism
An amiable, but scornful fellow worker in the Tuning department used to refer to shop stewards as shop stupids, a practice I found tantalizing, because he was no fool.

104   OUT OF TUNE

Changing Titles
The way the left wing political groups, continually changed their titles was remarkable. The Marxists / Communists, etc, became Socialists, Progressives, Stalinists, Maoists, The Broad Left, Engineering Voice, Workers Socialist League, All Trades Union Alliance, and many more. It seemed to me that every time a title was recognised as being a cover for Communism or Trotskyism, it took on a different title.

The Show Bay
For the final ten years of my employment at the Cowley Assembly plant, I worked in the Show Bay which was the department where the cars were prepared for the international and national motor shows, also VIP cars and special products. This was a job that occasionally involved a complete departure from the run-of-the-mill, factory work. I attended motor shows in Amsterdam, Brussels, Geneva, Cannes, Paris and Provdiv (Bulgaria), while colleagues went to Turin, Milan, Belgrade, Lausanne, Frankfurt and Barcelona. In the U.K. we covered Earls Court London, The National Exhibition Centre Birmingham, Glasgow and Bristol. I also did location work, when filming television commercials and other forms of publicity material in South Wales, the Cotswolds, Windsor Great Park, The South Bank Studios, and on Westminster Bridge. Also at Filming Studios at Shepperton, Chertsey, and on the old Brookland race track site at Byfleet. Finally an eight day session in the month of May, in Iceland.

One car that received VIP treatment was a Rover SD1 for Mr Arthur Scargil, the President of the National Union of Mine Workers. Another was for Oxford's Lord Mayor. That meant that at one time, I was helping to prepare the car for delivery, and some time later, it was being sent to our home to take Barbara, who by then was the Lord Mayor, and I, as her official escort, to attend civic functions.

I also took on a task that, at that time, for various reasons, other people, including supervision, had refused to undertake. It involved a number of new 2.7 Litre, V6 Honda, power-units, each valued at an estimated bought in value (cost to the company) of £3,000 for those fitted with a manual gearbox, and £3,500 for those with an automatic gearboxes. They were held in a secure compound, around which were many more units that had either faulty engines or gearboxes. The new units in the compound had accumulated for up to eighteen months, and had been cannibalised (robbed of parts that were not available from any other source). The urgency of the situation was because production of the current model was due to cease, which meant that the robbed units had to be rebuilt, and fed into the production system. Failing that, they would become obsolete stock and scrapped.

The actual task was to make good and to salvage as many power units as possible, before production ceased. My job also involved organising the facilities. I borrowed a wheeled high lift hydraulic appliance from the mechanical maintenance department, and was responsible for ordering the parts required from Tokyo. A task carried out by the stores staff on a daily basis. From time to, John Baines, a colleague from my old department (Tuning) would be sent to assist me. It was a job that suited me well. It meant I could do as much overtime as I liked, and on at least two occasions I worked while the rest of the factory were on a no overtime order, imposed by the management as a temporary cost cutting exercise. In the period of about five months, we rebuilt 120 power units of which 110 were fed back into the production system, yielding something in the order of £360,000 worth of recycled stock.

Other Peoples Books
In the book, *Inside Cowley* by Alan Thornett, the foreword was written by Ken Loach, a film maker of international repute (for covering such subjects as the plight of refuges who cross the border from South American countries into the Southern United States.). To illustrate Thornett's ability to influence an audience, Loach wrote the following. Quote - An argument is built up from a concrete situation that is immediately recognisable, and the audience is taken, step by irrefutable step, to the conclusion the speaker intends. End of quote.

Now I have been denied this wonderful experience, of being taken step by irrefutable step because he (Thornett) stubbornly refuses to address any meeting when I am present, in fact he has been known to refuse to open a public meeting until I have been obliged to leave. Far be it for me to suggest he fears that I might not succumb to the irrefutability of what he says. In fact, I am at a loss as to why he will not allow me to listen to what he has to say.

In a paragraph attributed to him on page 136 in *The Factory & the City* he attacks the Oxford County Council (OCC) and claims the T&GWU 5/293 and 5/60 branches represented 9,000 members at British Leyland, who have a policy of opposing public spending cuts and fighting for more, not less, nursery provision. That may, or may not, be right but he cannot possibly know. For a start, as the attendance at union branch meetings, where policies are adopted, is anything from 2%, perhaps as high as 10% of the combined branches' membership how then can he claim 9,000 votes for any policy? When OCC has dealings with comrade Thornett, they would be well advised to discount his figures on these matters by anything from 90% to 98% and Thornett must realize that to devalue his own word by uttering such exaggerations is an unprofitable practice. In truth of course, the percentages I have quoted apply to all sorts of issues, particularly on those that effect matters beyond the factory boundaries. From my knowledge of things, I doubt if more than 10% of the shop stewards, let alone the ordinary non-active members, attend branch meetings, and they are supposed to be the driving force behind everything.

On the bibliographical page of the book entitled *The Factory & The City* edited by Teresa Hater & David Harvey, there appears a dedication to the late Bob Fryer, with the comment *'who never gave up the struggle to save the*

Assembly Plant'. I would like either of the editors to supply me with the details of how and when Bob Fryer 'struggled to save the Assembly Plant'.

Having made inquiries from people who could be described as friendly towards Bob, the only answer to that question was that he supported the 'Save the Plant' (S.T.P) campaign that had been set up by the Oxford Trades Union Council. Further enquiries led to the fact that the S.T.P. campaign had failed to get off the ground and so it would seem that Bob Fryer was not able to conduct a struggle via that channel. I then asked how and why did the S.T.P. campaign fail, and it was explained to me that it was because the full time Union leaders refused to support the S.T.P., as they were meeting with the company. The factory union leaders were supporting Oxford City Council's 'South Works Closure' (S.W.C.) Committee campaign. The S.T.P. campaigners were invited to join the council s campaign which was supported by a much wider range of people and organizations, but they declined. So it seems that Bob Fryer backed the wrong campaign, which leaves me with the suspicion that Bob was never in a position to 'struggle' with anyone, therefore was the dedication out of place, even dishonest?

I can live with the fact that Bob Fryer has a cul-de-sac in the close vicinity of the BMW Factory named after him, because there were thousands of workers over the years that admired him, but there were equally as many that disagreed with him over the loss of jobs and debilitating strife that contributed to the gradual decline of what was once a great Oxford and national asset.

The following is an account of how I formed my opinion on Bob Fryer's performance and reputation from the late 1950's through to 1974. In other words, his first sixteen years of continuous office as the senior shop steward, of what was to become, the most powerful union in the factory. The trade unions had up until a few years earlier, had only a minority of the workers as members, and had very little influence with the management of the day. Consequently working conditions in thirty five year old factory buildings, and working practices that were as out of date as the buildings, the situation was ripe for demands by the unions, for management to make improvements all round, many were long overdue. To identify some of the issues included on the list was, better heating and ventilation, protective clothing, bonus payments, longer holidays, shorter working hours and the abandonment of paternalism. This meant substituting the length of service as the criteria for selecting people to fill vacant positions and the most controversial of all, was the demand for the implementation of what was known as the Movement of Labour agreement. In short, although everything and more, on that list could be justified over a period of time, it led to all sorts of unjustified and unbelievable demands and worse still, an almost continuous spate of wildcat (instant) strikes.

The amount of time the senior stewards spent, arguing with the management in those days was endless, and the culture developed where-by the leaders never ever to my knowledge, considered the effect of the endless demands and disruptive activities was having on the company finances. I will admit that when in attendance at large meetings of shop stewards, I was afraid to put an argument in defence of the company position even though there was a case for saying that we were destroying our own jobs. I would have been laughed out of court and achieved nothing. Though I did make the point in my O.R.M.O. leaflets that we delivered to the workers on the factory gates as they arrived for work.

So after more than twenty years, in the role of the demanding negotiator, in a position where the company were saying 'we are closing the plant, we don't need you any more', what exactly did Bob Fryer do, in his struggle to 'Save The Plant'?

A Dreamer
One person who contacted me, an ex Communist turned Trotskyist, said, 'I dont think we did any harm, do you?' 'You must be joking' I said. Where had this bloke been? New factories on green field sites closed down, (one of them held a fourteen week strike), and production switched to other factories after only five years existence. Famous, centuries old docks vacated and replaced by inland container depots - all because the union leaders of the day, having earned the support of their members for securing better pay and numerous other benefits, then turned to manipulating them into fighting the establishment. To change from capitalism to communism, using strikes as the method of attempting to gain control of the countrys wealth and, in so doing, trying to bypass the national electoral system. Obviously, he has not been where the action was

Luxurious runabouts
The management's most surprising economic measure was executed when they put at the disposal of the in-plant drivers, large luxury Honda Legend saloon cars that were to be used as hacks carrying spare parts, dirty spare wheels with punctured tyres, charged and discharged batteries, tools and towropes. In fact, anything that would have normally been carried in vans. It so happened the company had just renewed all of the vans that were used for the purpose described and the event was triggered by the fact that the Legends had been condemned for a sub-standard paint condition. The new vans were withdrawn and replaced with the Legends. It made sense of course because they were able to put the new vans onto the second hand market. It was interesting to note that the Honda people, to safeguard the good reputation, recorded the VIN (chassis) numbers and demanded evidence of the Legends destruction, having been scrapped within a pre determined date, thus ensuring they would never reach the second hand market.

Working on the night shift, I have a bad week.
Something I found extremely disagreeable was night work. Working one fortnight on dayshift and the next on nightshift and then repeating that, year in and year out, was not good. In fine weather, going to work while everyone else was preparing for an evening's recreation, and getting home in the morning, shattered and not knowing whether it is better to eat a meal before sleep, or sleep first and eat after. Vainly hoping there are no road repairs, or emergency service vehicles noisily thrashing by, or ice-cream sales vans plying their trade, perhaps having a nervous wife, stressed-out with fractious children to contend with through the night. These are the irritations when nightshift is being worked.

It was bad enough, having to work two weeks on nightshift and four weeks on days, which was my experience for seven years. No matter what I did, I would go to work on a Monday evening, reasonably well rested and cope quite well. On the Tuesday evening, I was not too pleased with life, and would find it tiring as my usual bedtime passed. By Wednesday, I knew I was losing ground on the energy side, the misery had to be suppressed, think of the long weekend, when it comes. God I hate bloody nights. Thursday evening, when I arrived for work, I was aware that it was the right night, but the wrong end. It was purgatory. The time dragged dreadfully, friends and fellow workers were bloody irritating. The supervisor could be a bit of a bastard sometimes. The tea breaks were hopeless. The first was from midnight to half past twelve. As I had craftily eaten my snack before the knocking-off whistle was sounded, I was able to get my head down straight away.

When the back-to-work whistle sounded I woke-up feeling like death warmed up. That was the first break over. The bloody job I was doing keeps going wrong. How come I never get it right first time? It will have to be taken apart, readjusted, and then reassembled. I hate this job. I had better speed up, otherwise that sarcastic bastard will come along with his unhelpful remarks. I remember him before he was promoted, when he asked me to cover for him when he was on some skive or other. Oh, the whistle's gone for the second break, it must be 3.30 a.m. I'll go and sit with old Bob and his little gang this break, he is a regular nightshift volunteer, they are usually good for a bit of lively banter. Not this time. Bob didn't seem to join in. It turned out that his marriage was going through a bad patch, according to one of his mates, she and the kids had gone back to stay with her mother, not for the first time, apparently. We are all back on our jobs, the 4 a.m, (end of the second break) whistle has gone, and being summer time, the first signs of daylight would soon appear. I begin to feel better.

I did get that problem sorted out in the end, but it was not possible to catch up the time lost. Nothing would be said about that. Things went quite well on the run-up to knocking off time. I finished the big job and had two more cars in with relatively quick jobs to be rectified. I sneakily washed up early, and kept out of sight for the last quarter of an hour.

It is Friday morning and the week is over. I had Friday, Saturday, Sunday and up until 8 p.m. Monday, before I started my second week of nights. I would still far rather have been on permanent dayshift. Throughout my seven years of working two weeks on and four weeks off, I never took a night off, purely because I did not like doing them. In fact, for the first couple of years of the nightshift operation, we used to work four of nine hour nights, and then four hours on Friday evenings from 5 p.m. to 9 p.m. to make up the 40 hour week, and I never missed any of them either. Barbara said that when it comes to work I am a masochist. How dare she!

A joke too far?
I am almost too ashamed to tell this story, but as it is true and perhaps, has a place as trivial history I will. It involved an incident, on nightshift, at about 4.45 a.m., when I was working in the Engine Change Section. I had nearly completed the task of changing the unit (the engine and the gearbox are joined together and referred to as the power unit) and had put the bulk of the lubricating oil into the gearbox and had done everything else that was required at that stage. I started the engine and was in the process of topping up the oil level (with the engine still running) through a very small filler tube. This took some degree of care to avoid missing the filler tube and making a mess of the engine and the floor. At this moment, one of the other lads, who went by the nickname of Pip, who had been watching me and larking about, put his hand on the engine throttle cable causing it to rev-up and down several times. This caused the engine to wobble (which was his intention, as a joke). This caused the oil from my oil measure, to spill and miss the aperture. After a couple of times I asked him to stop, but to no avail. I pleaded with him to stop, much to his and the other lads' amusement. I made one more plea. He continued his game and, in one quick movement, I swung the half full measure of oil round, and must have tilted it so that the bulk of the oil went from the top of his head down his face, into his shirt on down his front. I can still see him facing me, with the oil running down his face, calling me I-don't-know-what.

Pip, and a side-kick of his, a chap by the name of Les Birks (now deceased), started to walk away. I put the oil measure on my bench, only to find that Pip had turned around and was coming back, obviously still in a very angry state. Fisticuffs seemed imminent. So I once again took up the oil measure. Fortunately, that did the trick. Pip, with Les in tow, turned again and headed for the foreman's office. The outcome of it all was fairly predictable. A fight in the Tuning department was unheard of. George Hanks, the senior foreman in charge, was not the type to go by the book if he thought discretion would prevail. Nothing was ever said to me by the supervision or any member of management. He probably told Pip to sort it out between ourselves. George knew that to report the issue to the higher management would have left them with no option but to sack both of us for fighting.

I did wonder whether Pip and Les would be waiting for me outside the factory gates when we all went home, a little while later. If they had, I would have had a problem, because no-way would the security officer on the gates have allowed me through, carrying a recharged one-gallon oil measure. Back on dayshift, Pip and I were not on speaking terms for a couple of weeks. Our mates played on it for a while, then when we lifted the no-speaking ban, it allowed the lads that knew about it one last chance to give an almighty cheer.

Having described my own attitude towards the experience of working nightshift, I need to acknowledge that the variation in how it effects other people is wide. There is a significant minority of people who prefer nightshift working and that is something of a blessing, because it reduces the number of people, who have to. I felt quite indebted to them. There was also the difficulty of having to accept the belief that the problem was 'all in the mind'. However, having had a seven-year period of nightshift working, a change in the production schedule resulted in a reduced requirement for the two-shift system, and our department once again became a, day shift only area.

Some considerable time later, a night shift was re-introduced and, inexplicably, when the time came, I found that my abhorrence of nightshift had diminished, to the point where I actually voluntarily, worked a fifth night (overtime, from Friday evening to Saturday morning) on a number of occasions.

CHAPTER TWENTY-ONE
More Publicity

Publicity via the upper echelons of the industrial correspondents.

The Sunday Times 29 March 1981. Before Mr Rupert Murdocks ownership, on the front page of the Business News Section, was the heading, '*The Japanese juggernaut — the British road to ruin. The same job but worlds apart.* It featured a report by Roger Elgin in London, and Robert Whymant in Tokyo. It compared the differences between the working practices, conditions, attitudes and remuneration, of the two cultures through interviews with Kikji Karahashi, aged 35, a Datsun car worker, and Roy Gatehouse, aged 51, a Leyland car worker. They ended their seventy-column inch article and four large photographs, with the closing statement: *As for the past, Roy Gatehouse looks back on twenty-five years as a part of Britains car industry and passes stern judgement. 'We have wasted lots of opportunities and made lots of mistakes.'* My contribution to that article was the interview that lasted for ninety minutes and was conducted in my home.

Another feature by Roger Elgin in an equally prestigious publication in 1983, started: *Like a sudden thunder storm, the washing-up strike at BLs Cowley plant sprang from nowhere.* The unions had not anticipated it and when it came to the decisive mass meeting of the workers, for them to strike for a month over six minutes a day washing-up time certainly seemed an act of industrial suicide. Again, my contribution was another ninety-minute interview, in my house, culminating in an article of two thousand words.

Thornett's brand of Trotskyism equals Walter Mittyism. The following is a list of people and organisations that he opposes. He is against the Tories, the Labour Party, the Communist Party, the Workers Revolutionary Party, the police, Stalinists, British newspapers and other forms of media, political right wingers and moderates, full-time trade union leaders of his own trade union and others, the House of Commons and the House of Lords, entrepreneurs, Oxford City Council, Oxfordshire County Council, company directors, managers, anyone who operates within the capitalist system, consultative committees, and donkeys, especially donkeys! They are all traitors or worse in his eyes. I think he would be against Leon Trotsky if he were alive today. After all, he wasn't a shop steward.

Thornett likes shop stewards, not all shop stewards, I know that from experience, just the ones that agree with him. His faith in some shop stewards as defenders of the working class is confirmed by the last sentence of his book, *Inside Cowley*, where he roundly condemns the national officers of the unions and says, 'It's hard not to quote Arthur Harper, who said, they (the shop stewards) are Lions led by Donkeys (the national officers of the trade unions)'. Arthur Harper was known for being a 'loose cannon' who supported various revolutionary groups.

So there it is, Thornett reckons that industry and the government should be run by lion-hearted shop stewards.

I have a document titled *History of Trotskyism in Britain*. It has no statement of origin and can only be studied with that fact in mind. The first impression one gets is of the almost absolute instability of revolutionary institutions in Britain over the period of time covered by the document. It starts by saying that the first group arose in the Communist Party in 1931 and was expelled. The latest date mentioned is 1962. It is a list of divisions, other groups, new parties, personality clashes, exposures, changed allegiance, truces, dissolutions, splits, and a reference to Stalin's reign of terror.

The question that keeps popping up in my mind is why Leon Trotsky? He was never the president or prime minister of a small country, let alone a world power. Silly people from time to time identified other world figures as examples of better leaders of a more successful system of government, such as Stalin, until Khrushov exposed his reign of terror and until the Hungarian uprising. Then those same people switched to Chairman Mao and said Maoism was what we should all look to. What rubbish!

Leon Trotsky was no 'has-been', he was more of a 'never was'. Erstwhile communist supporters are all at sea since the demolition of the Berlin wall and the abject failure of the communist Russian State. The minuscule band of Trotskyists wrecked the image of communism in Britain. The communists were a party that offered the British electorate an alternative system, one that is radically left of the Labour Party and, as a pressure group, sometimes added their weight to causes that were accepted in parliament. Their general theme is for a better deal for the poor and under privileged, which fits in well with another aim of theirs, to level down the wealth of the rich. Surely there is some good in that. They led the fight against apartheid in South Africa a whole generation before other organisations saw which way it was going. Only then did the other organisations publicly support the cause and have since embraced Nelson Mandela for his leadership.

I question the logic of the militants thirty-year campaign against British industries, heavy and otherwise. Admittedly, the Trotskyists weren't the only ones to blame. Locally, they can rightly claim to have led the campaign from the front and were so far ahead they were almost out of sight. The ordinary shop stewards had a job to do, and that was to fight for their members' rights in terms of pay, working conditions, working hours, holidays, etc.

There is a clear line between industrial militancy and revolutionary politics. The latter has no place in factories and industries in general because it drags in the government of the day, the police, and, ultimately, the British army. We have all known the military to handle cargo in the docks, man fire engines, and drive ambulances. That is bad enough, but when it comes to private industry, the tactic is to let the industry die by pulling out and letting the foreigners take the trade. The danger for the ordinary worker is that, because these measures are not visible, when they go back to work at the end of a strike they think nothing has happened. In a very short time they will be squaring up for another fight, unaware that the employer will have already made plans to sell-up, 'downsize' or put the work out to contract. This all adds up to the need for able union leaders to know how far to go with their demands and the action they take in the pursuit thereof.

The logic behind what the union leaders did for so long, which was to deliberately sap the company's financial resources, made no sense. How could it possibly be advantageous to the workers, or the unions for that matter, for the company to be constantly short of money? Did these union leaders think the companies would get fed up and eventually hand over control to the shop stewards and the unions? How would that work?

In truth, the near closure of the whole factory provided a get-out for Thornett and co. because they were excluded from the task of restructuring the company but were still in a position to blame all and sundry for its difficulties. It enabled him to continue his role as a minuscule Leon Trotsky, whereby he could carry on propounding a theory without ever having to prove its viability. In the meantime, without the involvement of the Trotskists and their followers, a factory employing up to 4,000 workers remains and there is not an effective Trotskyite among them. The people who were part of, and led, the constructive approach in response to the dilemma, whether to close the whole factory or salvage a much smaller operation, was the Oxford City Council. It set up an Oppose the Closure Committee. It was made up of city councillors, Rover trade union representatives, a County Council representative, someone from the university, the church, someone from the local business fraternity and a community group representative. No business representative ever attended and a community group representative was never appointed, on the grounds that it was otherwise well represented.

Oxford and District Trades Union Council (which was back under the control of the militants) wanted to join the Oxford City Council's committee to oppose the closure of the factory. However, at a meeting, the Rover trade union shop stewards were opposed to the militants from the Trades Council being allowed to attend. When it was put to the city council's meeting, they were told they could have an observer with no right to speak. The Trades Council observer was then told that there should not be two campaigns against the closure of Cowley, and the Trades Council should disband their campaign and join the Council's committee. The upshot of it was that the Trades Council's observer was asked to stand down from the committee until he could unequivocally state that the Oxford and District Trades Union Council was not involved in a separate campaign against closure. The Trades Union Council decided not to disband and so was no longer part of the Oxford City campaign. In the end they did nothing.

The Oxford City Council financed the setting up an Independent Inquiry into the Rover Cowley Works Closure Proposals, to be chaired by Lord McCarthy of Headington. This included Tony Cristopher CBE, Sir Monty Finniston FRS, Dr Derek Morris and the Right Revd Patrick Rodger.

The Cowley Body Plant was reprieved and earmarked for a massive modernisation programme (much of which has been completed). A training school has been built and established and the old Assembly Plant site is being redeveloped with provision for a whole range of industries.

Whether by design or accident, the whole of the infamous Cowley Assembly Plant was obliterated, including all of the North side and the whole of the South side as well as the vast area behind Johnsons Café. The Body Plant site, where there was considerably less industrial strife, has been the object of a massive investment programme designed as a state of the art car producing facility. Surely that is pure symbolism.

Thornett was not a disaster, he was a tragedy, the consequences of which will be borne by thousands of people well beyond the factory perimeter, and will cover the whole area for years after us older ones have all passed on.

I always followed a policy of refraining from commenting on other workers' strikes if they did not immediately affect our factory. However, on one occasion, when our transport drivers were on strike on the very same day when Mrs Carol Miller and her close assistant, Mrs Wiffen, first led the Cowley Wives to protest at the factory gates, I was invited to the ITV studios at Birmingham to speak out against the people who were causing so much unrest. On arrival I was ushered into the building and introduced to a Mr Eddy McGarry, a senior shop steward at Canley, the Triumph Cars factory, whose role was to defend the militant activity. When I made the point to him privately that we, at Cowley, had suffered a one third loss of wages through strikes over the previous six months, he replied quite triumphantly, '*we have lost half of our pay over that period*'. I was at a loss how to cope with that attitude and went on to give the weakest case ever put on a live television programme. Fortunately, the events at Cowley, the wives march to the factory, eclipsed my effort, which I hoped was barely noticed.

In *The Factory & The City,* in a contribution on the closure of the Assembly Plant, Thornett chose to interpret the fact that neither Donald Stokes, Micheal Edwards nor the government, closed the Assembly Plant while the revolutionaries were in control. He wrote, '*We were told that the industrial militancy in Cowley and the left-wing leadership would lead to the closure, it never happened. Closure came with the right-wing leadership.*' If the reader of his book at this point were to look outside, he/she could be excused for thinking they caught a fleeting glimpse of a number of pigs flying past the window! It's a phenomenon that goes with the Thornett account of industrial history. They should take no notice; both are equally ridiculous.

He says the working class as a whole determine their own destiny and, in the same breath, blames all and sundry for their downfall. In 1979, after the defeat of the Labour government, and even more so in 1983, the working class voted for Margaret Thatcher, after she had carried out all sorts of measures against the trade unions. Going in to work after those general elections, I could find hardly any one who admitted they had voted Conservative. It seems the working class voters play their cards close to their chest.

A Different Union Leader, with a different style
Much has been said about a wide spread of people in this book, and one should not omit the name of someone because he left the scene (retired) back in 1982. His name and photograph was never blazoned across the local newspaper, let alone the nationals, for leading a strike that threatened the earnings of thousands of workers. He didnt work that way. His arena was the conference room, his working hours sometimes had little to do with the clock. Reaching agreement could take all day and half the night, in time to give the striking workers the earliest chance to get back to work and the wages to flow again.

The person featured in this statement has much to say, but says it quietly. He rose to high office in his trade union and, having started work at the Cowley Car Body Factory in 1937, had forty-five years experience to equip himself to the task of promoting the interests and welfare of the workers he represented. Between 1942 and 1946, his service was interrupted by a four-year break when he served in the Royal Air Force.

He took over the leadership of the Transport and General Workers Union from the legendary Josh Murphy, and in so doing, continued a policy that produced the highest paid workers in the area. *Mind you*, he said, when talking to me recently, *they had to earn it. It was piecework in those days and that was what the workers wanted*, and the factory thrived. With the ending of piecework in the early 1970s, the highest paid status was cancelled out. He told me his priority remained. *The T&GWU members interests came first and the company after that*. It never occurred to me to articulate such a statement, it was alien to anything I had ever encountered in my thirty-four years involvement in the Cowley Car Assembly factory.

Unfortunately, he was not our leader. He had no jurisdiction over our factory and could do no more than keep the Trotsky Revolutionaries in his domain from manipulating his members into anarchy and chaos.

The person I am describing is Bill Roche.

For three years Bill was a member of the T&GWU Executive Committee. He was on the National Automotive Committee, Joint Secretary of the National Participation Council and, for many years, until he retired, the Senior Shop Steward at the Cowley Car Body factory.

CHAPTER TWENTY-TWO

Finally

The decision by BMW to buy-out parts of the Rover Group in 1998 seemed to falter from time to time. Fortunately for Cowley a deal went through, with the result that hundreds of millions of pounds were invested in the old Pressed Steel site, which assured thousands of jobs for the local community. Even after BMW had committed themselves to develop the plant into a highly technical and advanced car producing unit, there were still major obstacles to overcome.

One obstacle was the need for the eventual, all-important, round-the-clock seven-day week to be accepted by the men and women who had to operate the system. I would have found that extremely difficult and have much sympathy with the workers faced with that working pattern, but I am contemplating the matter from the position of someone who is now seventy-one years old, when the ability to apply prolonged physical exertion and mental endurance diminishes considerably. My sympathy extends to wives, partners and offspring, who have to learn to live with a breadwinner who is working permanently either until the small hours of the morning or over the whole weekend.

The realities of life called upon us all in the past. In 1957 there was a forty-four hour week, with only one two-week annual holiday and six bank holidays each year. Added to those limits was a rule that if anyone unofficially extended the bank holiday, by taking an extra half or whole day, they forfeited the holiday pay. Us 'old uns' knew about inconvenience. For a start, the norm, when the factory was running efficiently, was to start work from the moment the hooter sounded, and to work continuously until lunchtime. The same pattern was expected after lunch until the hooter sounded at the end of the day. Those who were asked in June 2001 to operate the continuous production system have now accepted the challenge. This method is (a) necessary for BMW to compete with other car producers and (b) will yield a hard earned level of wages that in some quarters will be quite enviable.

The prospect of a healthy future for BMWs needs with regard to employment in the Oxford region looks good. Firstly it will be relatively easy to maintain 4,000 employees (when in my day up to 25,000 were employed between the two factories) and, secondly, because of the relatively high rates of pay BMW has to offer. This situation enables a selective approach to recruitment. In the past when Leyland were taking on as many as five hundred people for an expanding programme, the criteria seemed to be that if an applicant could stand on his/her feet for a day, attend regularly and was reasonably healthy, they got the job.

The last thing a company wants is to have employees who, once they are in, are fireproof and can join any group of strike-happy malcontents who, through inability or an unwilling attitude, neglect the commitment in return for the high wages they sought when they applied for the job.

It was some weeks after the workers accepted the 'Pay and Working Conditions' deal, which had attracted so much attention by the local media who had all covered the event in their news bulletins. Anything of that magnitude that happens at the factory usually arouses my interest and this was no exception. It was some time later that I contacted Bernard Moss, the T&GWU deputy senior steward, which turned out to be a useful way for me to catch up on the massively changed situation from the time when I retired in March 1991. None of the closures or demolition of the Assembly Plant had taken place then, and there was still production on both the North and South sides of the factory. By then the revolutionaries were floundering around.

There is no doubt about it, BMW, because of the competitive state of the car manufacturing industry world-wide, have been forced into the position of having to maximise the use of the massively expensive robotic apparatus, by operating it continuously, week in and week out. Perhaps ordinary people forget that the cost of investments continue when the plant is idle. Payments do not stop when all the workers are at home.

Of course, this fact was not lost on the three people on the Trade Union side whose job it was to negotiate terms on very little detail of the 'Pay and Working Conditions' package.

In order of rank there was Ivor Braggins, Tom White, and Bernard Moss. Ivor is the T&GWU District Secretary for the Worcester and Oxford region, a paid union official. Tom White is the Senior Shop Steward and Bernard Moss the Deputy Senior Steward, both employed and paid by BMW.

Ivor worked and was active in the trade union at the Cowley Assembly Plant from the early 1970s until he took his present position as full time union official. For most of that time, he was an ardent supporter of the late Bob Fryer, who for many years was the senior steward, when the unions led the most disruptive period in the seventy-five years since William Morris opened up the Cowley site. At one stage Bob Fryer was worried that Ivor, who was standing as a candidate in an election was 'in' with the Trotskyists. However, the next thing I knew, Ivor had cast off that allegiance. When Ivor and I met in the factory, instead of us having face to face arguments on the basis of Fryer versus the Moderates, Ivor would lecture me on the merits of moderation, to the point where I could hardly get a word in edgeways! Anyway, as if to emphasis the nature of his new commitment, he told me he was campaigning for Bill Morris in the election for the national office of General Secretary in the Transport and General Workers Union. Bill was the anti-revolutionary candidate and won that election and often appears in TV news bulletins. So Ivor had become 'one of us'.

Tom White was thought to have been a member of the Workers Revolutionary Party, but in my own contact with him over the years, I never saw anything of that kind. I know that he was very angry with Thornett over a number of issues.

Last, but by no means least, is Bernard Moss, who told me that he was quite happy to be deputy to Tom, and that Tom was, in his view, the essential member of the negotiating team. Bernard said he would ask Tom if he could find time to talk to me, but Im afraid no response meant it did not happen. Bernard told me a story about himself that I thought spoke volumes. It came about after he had worked for some years at the Cowley factory, some of which he had served as a shop steward, and he decided to take a break from factory life and went for something different. The experience did not come up to expectations and, as the Cowley factory were not taking people on, he had to settle for a job with Osberton Radiators, part of the Leyland combine at the Woodstock Road factory. Three months after he started there, he was nominated as shop steward, but when the process reached the stage where the management had to recognise this status, they refused on the accepted rule that an employee had to have one years service with the company to become a shop steward. Arguments on the issue at factory level failed to resolve the matter, and so the union side called for David Buckle, who, at that time was the District Secretary, to be brought in to put the union's case. The upshot of it all was, having pointed out to the management that Bernard had gained years of experience as shop steward at the Cowley factory, David pressed the management into dropping their objections and to grant Bernard official shop steward status, which they did.

Some time after this event, Osberton Radiators had to reduce their workforce and were transferring people to the Cowley car factory where there were then vacancies. Bernard heard about it and asked if he could be moved back to Cowley. The management refused. Bernard asked why and was told it was because they wanted him there. It turned out that, because Bernard was reliable in his work, a good time-keeper, had an excellent attendance record and generally observed all the rules, they were releasing people who lacked some of these qualities. More arguments ensued, but to no avail. Management had had the last word on the subject, or so they thought.

Bernard had other ideas. He started to break a few rules. First he went and stood by the clock early and waited for the finishing hooter to sound, a forbidden practice in that factory, and he systematically broke all the rules he had previously observed. It was not long before a member of management asked what was going on, what was he doing? Bernard explained that he wanted to get back to Cowley and he expected them to release him, and they did. What is more, Cowley took him back.

Bernard Moss was once involved with the Trotskyist movement. I suspect that he and others who joined them, did so because they, the Trots, have a positive approach to the inequalities between the privileged better-off people, and the socially and financially deprived in our society. There is nothing wrong with that, but Bernard, as with most of the other people who started going to their meetings, rapidly saw through the utter clap-trap that is dished up in terms of their operation and objectives. A few students swallowed their rhetoric for a term or two, but the small band of dreamers have got no real following by ordinary people. When the Trotsky movement was set up in Oxford, a few well-known trade union activists, including one local full-time union officer, attended the first meeting but never went again. One or two of those who did go were uncomfortable when the meetings kicked off by singing The Red Flag' (the international socialist song). Also sizeable weekly payments were expected from people who became members and they were also expected to sell their regular publications.

This team of three - Ivor, Tom and Bernard - in the process of vetting and easing the terms and conditions put forward by BMW, as their requirement from the workers, argued for ten hours over a period of three months, and some will say that BMW should have made further concessions, but they would not and that was finally accepted by the workforce in a vote at a mass meeting. The militants would have had either a strike or an overtime ban, for nothing, because no-one would have supported it for more than a week or two and they would have been going back to work a defeated and poorer force. Perhaps the union members have finally got the message, that an unviable strike damages everyone, and that they now work for a company that has shown more absolute financial and boardroom commitment and ability at Cowley than any other since the end of the Second World War.

The Trades Union and the employers, especially with the British built and originally conceived BMW Mini, I am sure, at last, are in the ascendancy, and I wish them well.

Name Index

Adams, Cyril 3
Arnold, John 82, 85-9

Baines, John 105
Bayliss, Lawson 73-4, 77
Birch, Reg 78
Birks, Les 109-10
Black workers rights 37
B.M.C. Service 7
B.M.W. 103, 113, 116
Bradley, Jim 34
British Leyland 2, 26
Brown, Andy 41
Buckle, David 28-9, 100, 118

Christopher, Tony, C.B.E. 28, 111
Coxon, Mr 37

Davis, Les 16, 68
Denver, Micheal 7, 17-8,
Dickson, Douglas 96
Duffy, Terry 46

Edwards, Michael 110
Eglin, Roger 111

Finiston, Monty, F.R.S. 111, 114
Fryer, Bob throughout

Gatehouse, Barbara 8, 17, 72, 81
Gibbs, Monty 35

Hall, Terry 82
Hammond, Charles 35-6, 85
Hanks, George 109
Harper, Arthur 112
Harvey, David 105
Hayter, Teresa 105
Heath, Edward 42
Hobbs, Doug 29, 78-9

Jackson, Brian 8, 85
Jeffcote, Alan 82
Jefferies, Roy 77, 80

Kikjl, Karahashi 111
Kinnock, Neil 8
Krushov 112

Landon, Harry 8, 35, 82, 85-6
Loach, Ken 105
Leonard, Lord 89

Margaret, H.R.H. Princess 6
Marston Coaches 2
May, Phillip 8, 35
McCarthy, William, Lord 1, 5, 12, 14, 114
McGarry, Eddy 114
Millar, Carol 46, 114
Morris, Derek, Dr. 111
Morris Motors 7
Morris, William 114
Moss, Bernard 114-8
Moss, Clifford 17
Murdock, Rupert 118
Murphy, Joss 115

Oxford Journal 78-9
Oxford Mail throughout
O.R.M.O.-T.U. throughout

Parker, Ken 74
Parsons, Reg throughout
Patel, 22

Radio Oxford 22, 43, 76
Roche, Bill 115
Rodger, Patrick, Rt. Revd. 114

Scanlon, Hugh 24, 46, 55
Scargill, Arthur 104
Smith, Andrew, Rt. Hon., M.P. 101
Soanes, Mick 28
Stalin, Joseph 104
Sturges, Peter 22, 24
Symonds, John 99

Thatcher, Margaret, Lady 13, 115
Thomas, Jack 3
Thornett, Alan throughout
Trinder, Percy 73
Turner, Graham 92
Trotsky throughout

Ward, David 82
Weakley, David 34
Wietz, Herbie 34-5
Whiffon, Margaret 31, 115
White, Tom 117-9
Wilson, Harold, Rt. Hon., M.P. 73, 79
Whymant, Robert 111
Wright, George 73

Young, Malcolm 8, 28, 29 78, 82-4